Beginner's Guide to Super 8 Film Making

GW00683543

Beginner's Guides are available on the following subjects

Cameras
Photography
Processing and Printing
Super 8 Film Making

Audio
Building Construction
Central Heating
Colour Television
Computers
Digital Electronics
Domestic Plumbing
Electric Wiring
Electronics
Gemmology
Home Energy Saving
Integrated Circuits
Radio
Tape Recording
Television
Transistors
Woodturning
Woodworking

Beginner's Guide to
Super 8
Film Making

Frank Arrowsmith

Newnes Technical Books

Newnes Technical Books

is an imprint of the Butterworth Group
which has principal offices in
London, Sydney, Toronto, Wellington, Durban and Boston

First published 1981

©Butterworth & Co (Publishers) Ltd, 1981

British Library Cataloguing in Publication Data

Arrowsmith, Frank
  Beginner's guide to Super 8 film making.
  1. Cinematography – Amateurs' manuals
  I. Title
  778.5'3491   TR851

  ISBN 0-408-00509-2

Typeset by Butterworths Litho Preparation Department
Printed in England by Fakenham Press Limited, Fakenham, Norfolk

Preface

Most people buy cine cameras to make comparatively simple family records, though success in this field may make them more ambitious later. But even with the simplest films it is very little more trouble to compose something that will give pleasure for years ahead than it is to shoot reels of disconnected scenes. This book describes how to go about it.

The modern Super 8 camera, with its automatic exposure control and other electronic systems, has simplified the technical side of the job in many ways, though it has also introduced a few complications. It is necessary to know what you can expect it to do and how to avoid the pitfalls. The camera will be right nine times out of ten, but it is worth being able to spot the tenth time and knowing how to rearrange or override the system. I have included enough technical information for normal day-to-day working, and perhaps a little more; any less would have made the subject more difficult to understand. The final chapter reviews the types of apparatus presently available, to help in the selection of suitable equipment.

Nevertheless, much of the book applies to film making with cameras of any size. Throughout we refer to Super 8, but take this to include Single 8, its close relative; and the principles apply to Standard 8, 9.5, 16mm and even video cameras. The camera is a tool that can be used with greater or less skill. It is *you*, the brain and the eye behind the camera, who make the film.

F.A.

Contents

1

Skeleton and shape

Every film needs its skeleton and its shape. Like a book or a piece of music, it should have a beginning, a development, a climax and a close. There is no need to be excessively formal about this: after all, you are the person who has to be satisfied with the results. But it is pleasant when your friends find your films unusually interesting. In fact, if they do, you yourself will find that you can go back to them time and time again; otherwise you will lose interest in them quite quickly. Cine films call for, and repay, organisation. They are quite different from still photographs, and need different treatment.

Backbone

The backbone of your skeleton is the plot. Even intimate and informal family records need plots, though they can be quite simple. Otherwise you will have a bag of disconnected bones that you never bring out of the cupboard. It is only too easy to make an animated snapshot album with a cine camera, but it isn't very rewarding, and the result won't please even you for very long.

Of course, there is more to a skeleton than a backbone. Sliding straight down that is rather like going for a walk when your sole object is to reach the other end as soon as possible. Your film should be more like a walk for the pleasure of the journey. It will have for its ribs glimpses of the surroundings, and for its arms and legs diversions to look at objects of interest by the way.

In this way your film begins to acquire the shape it needs. Not only should the ribs and limbs expand and decorate the original idea, but they should help to carry the film forward. The result needs to be consistent within itself, and should not jump about from place to place without explanation. It should explain itself as it goes along, like a *Tom and Jerry* cartoon. Part of the shaping will probably need to be done after the film is processed, as we shall see later, but unless you have a fair idea of what that shape is going to be in the first place, you are unlikely to be as pleased as you should be with the results, or to find them satisfactory in later years.

Filling out

The muscle of your film is the action. This is what distinguishes a film from a slide show: the characters are often (though not always) moving. The movement must have a purpose. It is no good pointing your camera at your subjects and saying 'do something.' They will smile vaguely and wave their arms about, and the result will be horribly unconvincing. You have to arrange for them to do something first, and photograph them while they are at it. Each piece of action should add something to the shape and direction of the film – it should show the skeleton moving with a purpose.

The flesh on your skeleton is formed by the quality of the photography. Your Super 8 camera and the film it uses are the product of a great deal of optical, engineering and chemical skill, whether you have the most complicated model or the simplest. All can produce pleasing and effective films within the limits for which they were designed. But they cannot think for you. Yours is the eye behind the viewfinder, and yours is the finger on the trigger. It helps, therefore, to consider what your camera can be expected to do, and how you can best use its capabilities. There are usually several ways of photographing the same scene.

The adornment of your – by now – body beautiful takes two forms. First, it involves the presentation of interesting and illuminating detail, from the carved knob on the church door

2

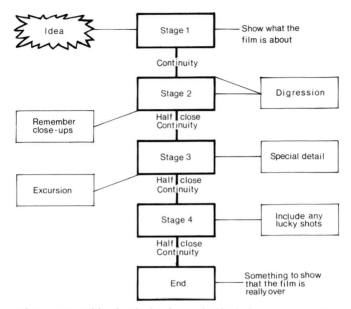

Whenever possible, decide the shape of a film before starting it. The classic pattern is easily shown in a flowchart

to the twisting hands of an excited child. Inspiration and the curious eye will help here.

Second, it involves such matters as titling – informing yourself and your audience about what is going on. Plain straightforward titles are useful, but so are other hints not so obviously contrived and added – posters, signs, famous views and sometimes actions. These add special interest to your films, and help to carry your audience with you through your experiences.

Editing

It is easy to see that some of your shots may have to be rearranged after your film comes back from processing. You would not think of showing anyone a set of still photographs in the exact order in which they were taken. You sort them first, throwing out the poor ones and putting the rest into some sort of logical order.

You do exactly the same with cinefilm. So do professionals, and almost certainly they throw away much more footage than you will. Your film, like theirs, will need cutting and editing before it can take its proper shape and make its proper impression.

You may already have some reels of film that don't seem to have worn very well. With a certain amount of editing and adornment, with a sorting out of the bone structure, they might be better than you think. The end result will not be as good as if the film had been planned from the start, but it can easily form a more entertaining record of the past than do the bags of bones. If you have the leisure and the inclination, sorting out the past can be an instructive guide to future filming.

Plan from the first

You want to interest yourself, and perhaps other people, in your films. Professional producers need to interest the public in order to stay in business. How, then, do they approach a production? They start by choosing a story, or theme, and from this they write a script. This contains not only the dialogue – which probably concerns most amateurs very little – but every little detail about the film. Not just stage directions, as in a play, but a meticulous description of each scene and each shot in each scene. Everything (costumes, camera angles, lighting and atmosphere) is written down before the cast are recruited and long before any photography starts.

We need not go to quite such lengths – we are not thinking of re-making *Gone with the Wind* – but are more likely to be concerned with making attractive records of our families, friends and surroundings. One approach to this is *A Day in the Life of* . . . someone or other, covering activities from getting up to bedtime – not necessarily, of course, filmed all on the same day. Similarly, you can make a record of a one or two-day event, such as a vicarage fete, in which family and friends are concerned. This could reasonably include some account of preparations, and the first draft note might run something like this:

Title: St Swithin's Fair, 1980
  1. Site
  2. Preparations
  3. Opening
  4. Stalls
  5. Events
  6. Closing

Not very informative so far, but now we go into more detail. To do this we consider, first, how the fete is actually put together. Apart from committee meetings, which are not usually very photogenic, there comes first the preparation of goods for sale, then the organisation of stalls and sideshows. Next the stall positions have to be allocated, and on or just before the day itself stalls and tents have to go up. After that we can go on to the show itself, but there is enough material to think about for the moment.

We want to start with a strong positive shot, and we must also try to find some sort of continuity link to keep the film flowing. We might do this by opening with the vicarage gates upon which some central character – the vicar, for example – is pinning a poster for the event. This can be followed by a view through the gates of the garden – not too long this time, because we are going to see a lot more of it later.

Select the details
From this we can cut to some of the preparations going on in homes and perhaps in the church hall. Here, lighting may be difficult and it might be as well to use a fast film (see page 28). One of the advantages of Super 8 is that you can change films before they are finished, losing only a few frames; but if you do, note the position of the footage indicator on the camera before you take the film out, because it automatically goes back to zero every time you change.

There will be people sewing or producing handwork, making jam, cakes and pickles, and perhaps growing and picking vegetables and flowers. With a bit of persuasion you can get at least some of the indoor activities posed near good windows, or even outside if the weather is good. Some shots you may get from the outside looking in, so that you photograph the most brightly lighted side. In that case make sure your camera is adjusted to the light *inside* the room and not to that on the wall and window frame (see pages 34 and 75). Some, but not all, of these scenes should introduce the vicar calling to see how things are going.

Now we can cut back to the vicarage garden and show a group going round siting stalls. There might be some mimed – or even, if you are using sound (Chapter 9), recorded – argument: '. . . but I *always* have my stall under that tree!' This could lead directly in to the delivery of stall and sideshow materials, with various pictures of people putting them up. Indeed, you might be able to go back a little and show carpenters working on the actual construction of the stalls.

The event itself
At last the stage is set for the event itself. The gates open, the visitors come, the opening ceremony takes place, and then

A film of a simple event needs very careful planning to include all its aspects, with little chance of reshooting. A variety of shots adds considerably to the interest

we can attend to the activities of the day. Unless there is a particularly interesting person or action involved, you may not want to spend long on the actual ceremony. A short piece showing the end of a speech and some clapping – sound again, if you are recording it – should be enough; then you can move to the stalls, the sideshows, the raffle or whatever else is going on. Not, I suggest, in procession with the chief guests, though you could use some shots of their progress. You will want to have more variety than a straight tour allows, and you can produce this by cutting from a stall to a crowd view, to a sideshow, and to middle and close-up shots of people in whom you are especially interested. Your anchor man, the vicar, should appear from time to time, and so should some at least of the characters you used during the preparations. This will tie the whole thing together, so that you have a neat and flowing account of the event itself and of your friends and family.

To round it all off, you need a definite close, and that rather depends on what actually happens. If, for instance, there are fireworks you will want to show them. But a neat ending – which can, of course, be arranged and acted after the hurly-burly – would be to show the vicar shaking hands with the last guest, taking the poster down and closing the gate.

Storyboard
A film of this sort, and indeed many films you will make, cannot be written down in full detail. However, you will benefit enormously from thinking it through first, listing probable shots, to which any unexpected gifts from the gods can be added. So, for this purpose, you might note;

Title
Vicar at gate
Mary making jam
Aunt Sally sewing – vicar looks in
Joe picking tomatoes
Vicar, Joe and Mary in garden
. . . and so on.

Travel films

Another subject that provides its own beginning and end is a visit: your holiday or a visit to you, including a visit from a member of the family who is employed or at school away from home. But the simplicity of the framework – arrival and departure – may be deceptive. Too much footage about luggage, cars and trains becomes wearing, and it is the middle part about the actual holiday that counts.

Nevertheless, you will want to try the whole treatment at least once. The opening sequence for a holiday of your own could run something like this:

Strapping up the last case
Luggage at the door
Taxi
Arrival at the station
Boarding the train
Shots from the carriage window
Arrival at the airport
Boarding the plane
Takeoff
Leaving the plane
Arrival at destination

The trouble is that superficially all luggage, all taxis, all stations and all airports look much the same. And when you are making the journey yourself you have too many things to think about to spend much time filming. The meat of your holiday film should really be the place you are visiting.

Unless you are making a really leisurely journey, you may well find that it is better to delay filming until you get to your destination, and start with an establishing shot: a road sign, an airport notice or a well-known view like Big Ben or the Eiffel Tower, with a member of the party either standing about or in an obviously related shot immediately after.

Film with a purpose
Then what next? You have to make up your mind (preferably before you start) whether you are making a film about

yourself and your companions on holiday, or about the place you are visiting. The one need not exclude the other, but there is the question of emphasis. You can construct a valid film of your party doing whatever it is they have come to do, with just sufficient local background to identify the area, or you can make the area and its characteristics your subject and include your companions mainly incidentally but sometimes as principals.

If the emphasis is to be on the company, you will need to work out what they are going to do, and cover these various activities. However, if you find that your nearest and dearest tend to look much the same in holiday clothes (weather permitting) whether they are in Barbados, Benidorm or Blackpool, you may prefer to concentrate on the locale, while including enough family shots to make the film personal and to record what they looked like at the time. The following notes are based on this approach.

It pays to find out something about your destination before you leave. You will want to do this anyway, for the better enjoyment of your visit, but while you are studying your brochures and guides make notes – mental if you like, but better in writing – of places or events that look like film material. Then, on arrival, try to spend a day absorbing the local atmosphere and looking at your selected possibilities before shooting. But do not, in the process, miss unrepeatable shots. If the carnival parade is on the day you arrive, film it: you may find later that you could have done it better, but you have only the one opportunity.

Select your subjects for variety as well as for interest and local colour. If you can, try to see them in various lighting conditions as the sun moves round. Look at the local picture postcards: you don't want to copy them, but the subjects are presumably chosen because they are of interest, and they can give you ideas about angles of view. If you can find interesting corners that are not generally photographed, so much the better, but you also have to consider the time at your disposal and how much of it you are prepared to spend on photography.

9

Now you can make a working list of scenes. Assuming that you are at a seaside town, it might be something like this:

Arrival
Family, unburdened, enter promenade café
Promenade
Beach and coast: fishing boats leaving
Tour of town (by horse carriage? but don't film while
    moving: it will joggle your camera too much)
Castle or cathedral
Nearby countryside, with farmers
Carnival – if available
Fun fair – if liked
Bathing, beach football etc.
Fishing port: return of fleet and sale of fish (evening)
Sunset on beach: family come out of water
Close on darkening waves

The main joker in this pack is the tour of the town. Tours are usually available, and they take in the main places of interest. It does not follow that you take all your photographs during the tour. They can be taken at other times and fitted in afterwards. The tour itself is valuable link material.

Otherwise the family is the main link. They should appear frequently, though not always obtrusively. In fact, they need not actually be there all the time. If you precede and follow a shot of the cathedral with one of the family, going nowhere in particular, they will appear to have made the visit even though they were out swimming at the time, totally fed up with carrying tripods and camera bags.

There is no need to stick to the order of scenes I have suggested. It is simply an example of an orderly and logical sequence of events – arrival, exploration, more detailed examination, and evening activities leading to a gentle end. You can redesign it to include night lighting at the funfair and finish with a firework display. But you want a progression of events, and within that progression each separate sequence should have a unity of its own, like a chapter of a book.

Take for instance, the beach scene. This should show arrival, getting organised, testing the water, swimming, lying out to dry, castle building and so on, and finish gracefully with a retreat. The reason that I have suggested putting it at or near the end is that it links well with the return of the fishing fleet. Also the family leaving the water as night falls helps to suggest the end of the visit and of the film. You may wish to plunge everyone in after the promenade shot, which is quite logical, but in that case you will need either two beach shots, or a different ending. The great thing is to try to make each section come to a half close, rather than to an abrupt end followed by an abrupt start to the next subject. Keep the film flowing until you reach a full close at the end.

Journey films

If you believe (with Hazlitt) that it is better to travel hopefully than to arrive, you may be planning a tour of some sort for your holiday, or you may have the opportunity to make a necessary journey in a leisurely way. In this case your film can be about the journey itself.

Your trip might be by train, by car or, ideally in my view for film treatment, by water. Ideally, that is, because water travel is comparatively slow, and takes place on a normally steady vessel probably handled by a trained crew. You are therefore free to concentrate on your filming and have plenty of time to work out your shots. So let us suppose that you are travelling from London to Athens, calling at Lisbon, Gibraltar, Sardinia and Naples on the way.

You will want to record three types of scene: ship working, shipboard activities, and the look of the ports of call. You will also want some means of indicating the movement of the vessel between ports.

Embarkation being usually a slow business, you should be able to start with a quayside shot or two. The ship's bow, with her name, makes an effective beginning, followed by passengers climbing the gangway. Once on board, you can leave unpacking for a duller moment. You will probably find derricks or cranes still working with the last of the cargo or baggage, and you might want to take the quayside again from above, particularly if there are friends seeing you off. Then

11

there will be a group of flags at the foremast. The ship's house flag will be at the masthead, and on the signal halliards the International Code flags: P (the Blue Peter) and either the blue and yellow striped G, asking for a pilot, or the red and white H which means 'I have a pilot on board'. If you are on a British ship, the Red Ensign will be at the stern; if not, the flag of the ship's own country will be there and the Red Ensign at the aftermast.

Then you can film the ropes dropping away as you finally sail, and from the stern a view of the disappearing port. There is often a useful vantage point for this sort of shot on the upper deck; it is a little cage sticking out over the water

(A) Take plenty of continuity shots while travelling. They make ideal cutaways between more rigidly sequenced shots. (B) Beginning and ending a documentary with a travel shot helps to enclose the film into an impression of a single visit. (C) When recording the activities of a 'single day' a cutaway to a clock helps the film along

from the side, intended for the gentleman who measures the depth of the water with a leadline. It is rarely occupied by the crew these days, for ships have electronic devices to do the job, but it can be very useful to you. Indeed, your next shot – though not immediately – could be from here, of a bow wave to show movement. Bow waves and wakes do this very well.

We seem to have taken a long time getting under way, but this is deliberate, to show how you could build up that particular scene. Similar principles apply to all scenes: they should be connected to form sequences in themselves. With luck, for instance, on arrival at a port you can spot the pilot vessel coming out and possibly film the pilot climbing up the rope ladder to come aboard. This can be preceded by a shot of code flag G, and followed by G coming down and H going up. You can, if you are very smart about it, do this as a continuous sequence at one time. But a sound alternative is to film the pilot when you can and concentrate on the flags on another occasion, cutting them together afterwards, in the way described in the editing section.

At about this time, you can also expect to see the plain yellow code flag Q go up. This is commonly, but wrongly, called the quarantine flag. It is true that no-one is allowed ashore until it comes down, but its true meaning is 'My ship is healthy, and I require permission to land freely'. The quarantine signal requires two square flags and some triangular ones.

Next, shipboard activities. Well, there are deck games, the swimming pool, a visit to the bridge and perhaps a children's fancy-dress party, besides just sitting about with drinks and sometimes, in warm weather, meals on deck. Below decks, your cabin might be light enough for a shot with standard film, but the dining room will be too far down for shots of eating or dancing unless you use the fast Ektachrome or type G film (see pages 28 and 68).

All this will depend on the circumstances of the ship and the voyage. You will certainly wish to photograph something of all that is practicable, but the emphasis you give will depend on your personal interest. Deck games, for instance, with the possible exception of deck tennis, are not generally very photogenic, and their players are often notable for their enthusiasm rather than their skill. So your interest, and that of your audience, is likely to be satisfied by quite short shots unless you have a personal connection with the player. Similarly, the attraction of the swimming pool will doubtless vary according to the attractiveness of the swimmers. You will want to space shots of this sort at intervals between ports of call instead of all in a string. However, take them when available and sort the order out later in editing.

Following the route proposed (though I offer no guarantee that any such trip is available) you will be within easy sight of land in three places, apart from entering ports. You would pass through the Pillars of Hercules (the Strait of Gibraltar) and between Scylla and Charybdis (the Strait of Messina) before threading through the Greek islands on your way to Piraeus. In my experience ships have a habit of doing these bits at two in the morning or some such inconsiderate hour, but it would be worth finding out the times and trying shots if they looked useful. These, though, like many other shots would depend on the weather. There are times when the Strait of Gibraltar looks little wider than a lake in a park, and other times when you can't see across it.

At your ports of call, you would show enough of arrival and departure to make the point; unless there is something special about the procedure you will not want to treat them as fully as your original departure. Therefore, you can photograph the things about the port that are different – types of boats, styles of architecture and paving, and the way people behave. In Gibraltar there are the apes as well as the street markets; in Naples people hang their washing out to dry across the narrower streets. There will be excursions available, to Vesuvius and Pompeii for instance. But always keep an eye open for the odd detail – the woman at her stall, the man with the curious pipe, or the mosaic on the fountain. You cannot script this sort of thing in advance, unless you know a great deal about the places. You can only be ready to catch the fleeting moment.

Finally, you arrive at your destination. Here, you can afford to go into some detail about landing, and finish your film with as much as you want of Athens, concluding perhaps with a shot of the Parthenon against the sky.

Any other journey can be treated in much the same way. The interest of your film is going to lie less in the esoteric nature of what you have seen than in the quality of your photography and the way in which you put it together. So the following chapters discuss, with a little technical detail, how to use your camera to get the effects you want and make each shot interesting in itself, and then how to sort out the pieces so that they tell a coherent story.

2

Tools

What is a camera?

This may seem a silly question, but it helps to go right back to first principles from time to time. Centuries ago someone discovered that if you darken a room completely, a pinhole through the shutter will throw an image of the scene outside, faint but good enough to trace with a pencil, on to a screen inside. The device became known as a dark room or, in Latin, a *camera obscura*.

Now a room has but one view, and a pinhole does not let in much light, so the next step was to use a portable shaded box instead of a room and substitute a lens for the pinhole. This arrangement is said to have been first described by Giovanni Batista della Porta in 1569, but it is thought to have been in use much earlier.

When someone realised that certain chemicals darkened on exposure to light, the thought followed that instead of wearily tracing the image from a camera obscura on to paper, light could be made to do the job itself, and this use is accredited to Thomas Wedgwood in 1794. In any case, there we have the basis of the photographic camera – a box with a hole at one end and light-sensitive material (in our case, a film) at the other.

Photography today is based on chemicals that change on exposure to light, and in proportion to the quantity of light. Left for long enough, they darken, but after a very much shorter exposure they can be induced to change by reaction with other chemicals – by what is called *development*. This produces a negative, on which what was originally black is white, and vice versa. From this, prints are produced by using exactly the same process: the light passes through the film on to sensitised paper, which is then developed.

It is possible to produce films and slides in the same way, using film instead of paper, but at least for amateur purposes the original film is put through an extended process that changes the image back to what the eye has seen. This is called *reversal processing*. The production of colour is a matter of more complicated and ingenious chemistry, but the basic principles are the same.

The trick is to get exactly the right amount of light on to the film. Too much, and the image (when reversed) will be too thin and pale; too little and it will be extremely dark.

The still photographer has two means of control. By using the shutter mechanism he can expose the film for longer or shorter periods, and he can make the hole through which the light enters – the aperture of the lens – larger or smaller by turning a ring that opens and closes a device within the lens – the iris diaphragm – put there for just that purpose. Cine cameras, however, are different. The time of the exposure is controlled by the speed of the film passing through, and normally it is fixed at about $\frac{1}{40}$ second. A limited variation is possible on the most advanced cameras (see page 44), but in the main the only exposure control is the aperture of the lens. Most Super 8 cameras have an electronic device to adjust this, but let us first consider the lens itself.

How the lens controls the image

Lenses are described by two figures, one for focal length and one for maximum aperture. The focal length is measured in millimetres and is roughly (though not strictly scientifically) the distance between lens and film that produces the sharpest possible image of a distant object. The aperture is described by an '*f*-number', which is obtained by dividing the diameter of the lens into the focal length. The reason for

17

doing this sum rather than using the diameter itself is that it gives us a measure of the amount of light transmitted, whatever the focal length may be. Thus, while the effective diameter of a lens of 8mm focal length and *f*/2 aperture is 4mm, and that of a 40mm lens of the same aperture is 20mm, both will allow the same amount of light to reach the film; so the *f*-number is useful but the diameter is less so.

In both still and cine cameras, the actual aperture at which you expose is controlled by an iris diaphragm marked with *f*-numbers in the series 1, 1.4, 2, 2.8, 4, 5.6, 8, 11, 16, 22 and 32. Each number represents a hole that lets through half the

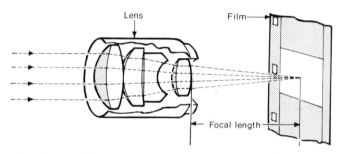

A lens forms a sharp image of a distant subject when set exactly one focal length from the film. In a zoom lens, the effective position of the lens alters with focal length to maintain focus

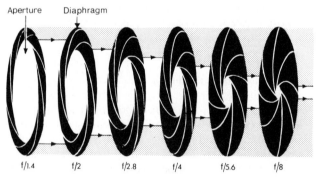

The lens diaphragm alters the brightness of the image by changing the size of the aperture through which the light passes

18

light that its predecessor transmits: the bigger the number, the less the light.

The effective diameter of the opening in a lens for any given aperture can be worked out quite simply: divide the focal length by the stop number. The standard focal length of fixed lenses when fitted to Super 8 cameras is about 12½ mm, in which case the 'hole' in an $f/2$ lens would measure 6¼ mm across. If the smaller apertures are considered in the same way, it becomes clear why cine cameras cannot be stopped down beyond a certain point. An aperture of $f/16$ requires a diameter of only 0.78 mm, $f/22$ requires 0.57 mm, and so on down the scale. On a wide-angle lens of 8 mm focal length, $f/16$ requires 0.5 mm, and $f/32$ (which is one smaller than usually supplied) only a quarter of a millimetre – impracticably tiny. The situation with a zoom lens is more complicated, but the same constraints apply. For this reason standard cine film is comparatively slow. Fast film is reserved for adverse lighting conditions (see page 28).

Focus and depth of field

As we have said, the focal length of a lens is the distance it needs to be from the film to produce the sharpest possible image of a distant object – for our purpose anything over about ten metres (thirty feet) away. Fortunately for photography, this is not the whole story. There is an area both in front of and behind the exact point of focus within which the images are acceptably sharp. The distance between the nearest and furthest acceptable point is called the *depth of field*.

Depth of field varies with both focal length and aperture: the shorter the focal length and the smaller the aperture, the greater the depth of field. Put another way, it varies according to the size of the hole you are using, irrespective of its light-passing qualities. The simplest still and cine cameras have small apertures, large depth of field producing reasonably sharp images of both close and distant subjects. In more advanced cameras the photographer adjusts aperture and focus to increase/decrease depth of field.

The point is that if you are shown a picture in which some parts are sharp while others are fuzzy, you naturally concentrate your attention on the sharp bits – provided, of course, that they constitute the main parts of the view. Supposing, therefore, that it is impossible or even undesirable to arrange a shot so that all irrelevant detail is outside the frame, it may still be possible to concentrate attention by focusing on the essentials and leaving the other things fuzzy. This is known as *differential focusing*.

Since standard lenses used in Super 8 cameras are of very short focal length, and have correspondingly long ranges of acceptable focus, differential focusing can only be used when zoom lenses are at long magnification positions, and when the light is sufficiently low as to require wide apertures. The technique, however, is essential in some circumstances in order to concentrate interest on the correct subject. Although natural lighting conditions may not always favour its use, we can apply the technique by reducing the light reaching our lens; that is, by introducing a 'neutral density' filter (page 71) so that the wider aperture does give the differential focusing effect required.

Effect of focal length
The focal length of your lens determines how much of the view will appear on your film from any given viewpoint. If you are in any doubt about this, remember that light rays travel in straight lines and cross over inside the lens. Think of two rods anchored a short distance apart and crossed through a ring. The distance from the plane of the anchor-points to the ring represents the focal length, and the rods the light rays. The longer the distance from anchor to ring, the closer together come the outer ends of the rods.

Standard focal lengths have been chosen for each size of film so that the resulting photograph includes what the eye can reasonably be supposed to include without moving. Shorter focal lengths make inclusive shots possible when things are crowded, as a large building is crowded in a narrow street; longer focal lengths concentrate the camera on interesting action farther away.

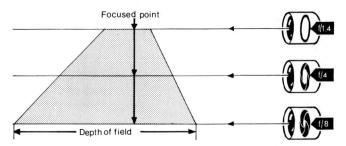

At the same focus distance and focal length, the smaller the lens aperture the greater the extent of sharp focus (depth of field)

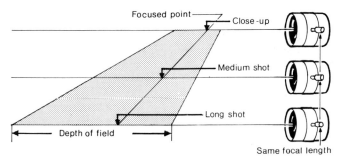

At a fixed focal length, the depth of field increases with focus distance

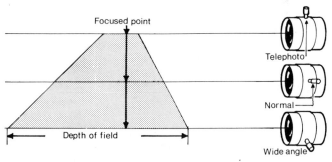

At the same aperture and focus setting, depth of field increases as the lens is zoomed to a wider angle

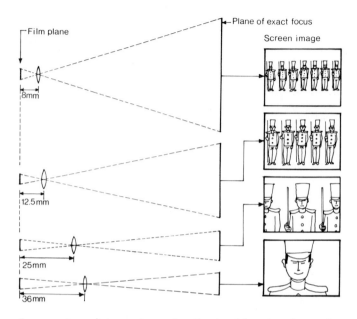

From a given distance, increasing the focal length enlarges the image, thus selecting a smaller subject area

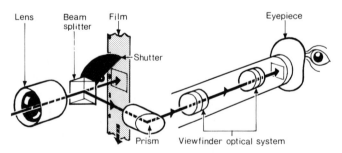

Zoom lenses are easiest to use with reflex (through-the-lens) viewfinders. A prism bleeds off some of the incoming light to offer an image that demonstrates exactly the image area and focus point. The lens diaphragm works behind the beamsplitter, so the viewing-image brightness is not affected by the aperture setting

Viewfinders

Naturally, all cameras have viewfinders so that you can see more or less accurately what you are taking. They are of two types. The first is an optical system quite separate from the actual working of the camera; the second, the reflex system, allows you to see through the taking lens even while it is in action.

There is no doubt that the second is the better of the two. Not only does it automatically take into account any change

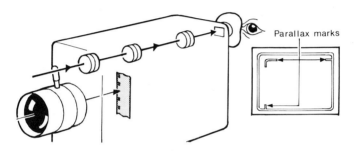

Parallax marks

Simpler optics are produced with a separate optical viewfinder. Coupled finders show the changing field of view as the lens is zoomed, but may not be as accurate as a reflex viewfinder. Marks in the viewing system allow you to compensate for parallax, i.e. its slightly different viewpoint when shooting close-ups

in the focal length of the lens, so that you can see just how much of the scene in front of you is included in the picture, but in many cameras (see page 41) it also allows you to see whether you are in focus. The separate optical system tells you nothing about focus, and requires some sort of mechanical adaptation, whether by means of engraving within the apparatus or by external shutters or lenses, to take account of different focal lengths. It is also slightly inaccurate at very close quarters. However, this system is, these days, usually only fitted to fixed-focus cameras (see page 31), which do not accommodate lens changes or very close-up work.

Reflex viewfinders and exposure

Reflex viewfinders on cine cameras work by extracting some of the light entering the lens before it reaches the film. In the middle of the lens there is a device that lets most of the light go straight on to the film, but reflects some of it on to a mirror and so through another series of lenses to the eyepiece. These lenses make up for the parts of the main lens through which the active light has still to pass after the extraction point; at the same time, they reverse the image so that it is the right way up in the viewfinder.

The only disadvantage of this otherwise excellent system is the loss of light, and this only matters in the more adverse conditions. It does not affect normal working at all, since the meter reading allows for the difference, but it does mean that a rather larger aperture is needed than would otherwise be the case, and therefore that the minimum light requirement is rather more. So the camera registers 'don't expose' in light that an equivalent lens with a direct optical viewfinder might find just sufficient. In fact, few reflex cameras can approach the low-light performance of the original (Kodak) XL non-reflex models, despite nearly ten years of development. But for practical purposes the difference is small, and the advantages of a reflex system well outweigh this handicap.

Film

It is confusing that the word 'film' is used both for the raw material and for the finished product: the context usually makes clear which is intended. In most of this book it means the finished product, but for the rest of this chapter it means the raw material.

Film, as everyone knows, consists of a transparent base coated with a light-sensitive material. It is sold in many shapes and forms, but for Super 8 purposes it comes as a strip 50 feet (15 metres) or occasionally 200 feet (60 metres) long and 8 mm wide with a row of holes down one side. There is one perforation for each potential frame of the finished film.

This is packed in a plastic cartridge, which completely encloses it except for a few frames on one side where the exposures will be made. The whole cartridge goes into the camera, and it is so designed that it operates (or does not operate) a switch that tells the exposure meter whether you

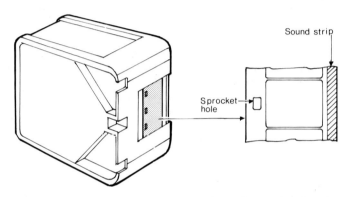

Sound strip

Sprocket hole

Super 8 film comes in quick-load cartridges. The notches key the camera's built-in meter system for film speed and colour balance. Striped sound film is available in either silent cartridges for later addition of sound, or sound cartridges for live sound shooting

are loading normal or fast film. Because of this construction it is possible to remove a partly exposed film (in order to substitute faster or slower stock) and to insert it again later with the loss of only a few frames. But when this is done it is important to note the reading on the camera's footage register, which reverts to zero every time a cartridge is removed. On completion, the cartridge is sent for processing either direct to the manufacturers or through your local dealer. The finished product comes back to you on a reel ready for a trial show.

Film speeds

In order to get our exposures right, we need to have some measure of the speed at which film reacts to light. Many systems have been devised, all of them expressing speeds as numbers. The two commonest are called ASA (American Standards Association, now the American National Standards Institute) and DIN (Deutsche Industrie-Norm).

In the ASA system, the figure is directly proportional to the speed of the film. If the speed of the film doubles, the index doubles, so in the same conditions a film rated at 25 ASA will need double the exposure of one rated at 50 ASA, or four times that of one rated at 100 ASA. Most cine film is rated at either 25 or 100 ASA in daylight conditions.

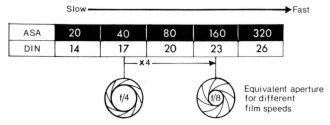

The faster the film, the smaller the lens aperture needed in any particular conditions

The DIN system works on multiples of 3: each increase of 3 on the scale represents a doubling of the film speed. A film rated at 15 DIN requires twice the exposure of one rated at 18.

These two scales have an equivalent point at index 12. The table below shows how they differ thereafter; speeds below index 12 are academic from our point of view.

ASA:	12	25	50	100	200	400
DIN:	12	15	18	21	24	27

Film types

There are three broad classes of colour film generally available, one for daylight, one for artificial light and one equally suitable (or unsuitable) for both. Filters are available to allow the use of daylight (type D) film in artificial light and artificial-light (type A) film in daylight. Type G is used without a filter under both conditions.

Type D need not detain us, for it is not available for Super 8 cameras, though it is for the older standard 8mm.

Super 8 cameras are designed for use with type A film; they have a built-in filter to convert for daylight. This filter is normally in position, and has to be swung out of the way when filming in artificial light. There are a number of methods of doing this, and details will be in your instruction book.

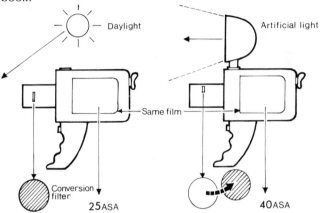

Virtually all Super 8 colour film is balanced for artificial light. Most cameras have a built-in orange filter to give good colour reproduction in daylight. This reduces the effective film speeds to 25 and 125 ASA. For work in artificial light, the filter is moved aside either with a switch or with a fitting in the light socket.

At first sight this seems upside down, for most of our filming is done in daylight, but there is a good reason for it. Conversion filters, like most others, call for an increase in exposure. Artificial light is much less intense than daylight, so it makes sense to use your filter in the brightest conditions and take it out when things are against you, thus getting the maximum speed from your film when the light is at its worst.

Also, the blue filter used for type D to artificial light conversion absorbs more light than does the amber one for the reverse process. Within type A there are three divisions:

(1) Standard – Kodachrome 40, Agfachrome and several others. These are the films normally used. They have a speed rating of 25 ASA to daylight and, filterless, 40 ASA to artificial light.

(2) Fast – Ektachrome 160, with speed ratings of 100 and 160 ASA respectively. These are used when there is insufficient light for ASA 25/40 films. They reproduce colours noticeably differently from standard films, and do not mix well with them in finished productions. But they are too fast for most cameras in bright daylight, so:

(3) Ektachrome 40 (ASA 25/40, as for Kodachrome) was made for use in bright daylight when a production is to include both day and evening or interior sequences. (The reasons for this are given more fully in Chapter 5 on low and artificial light). It is not, however, currently available everywhere.

Type G Ektachrome is a compromise film rated at 160 ASA for both types of light, and needs no filter in either of them. Thus you do not get bad patches through forgetting to adjust your camera to suit the type of light – unless of course you forget completely in the first place. On the other hand, it is very fast indeed for daylight use, and though the colour rendering is reasonably acceptable, not even the makers would claim that it is as accurate as that of the other types. Indeed, if it were possible to make a universal film that equalled the quality of types A and D, no doubt the makers would concentrate on that and jettison the rest. Because of the colour rendering, it is better not to mix type G with any other in a finished film.

One final point: Ektachrome films are cheaper in the shop than the standard sort, but more expensive to use because you have to pay extra for processing – it is not included in the price of the film itself. On the other hand, you can sometimes get them processed in those few countries where there are no Kodak laboratories.

How movies work

A moving film is the mechanised equivalent of those little
card booklets of drawings you sometimes see, designed so
that if you flip the pages over quickly the subject of the
drawing seems to be moving. A film is just such a sequence,
of photographs each slightly different from the last, projected so quickly on to the screen that you are aware only of

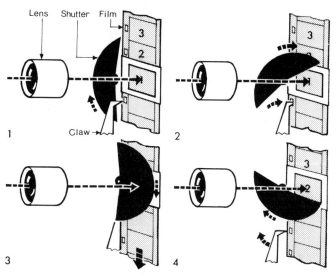

Light is focused on the stationary film when the shutter is open (1).
As the shutter closes, the film transport claw engages the film (2).
With all light excluded, the film is moved down exactly one frame (3).
As the shutter opens for the next frame, the claw disengages and
moves up to the next sprocket hole (4)

the total impression, and not of the separate frames.
Conversely, of course, a cine camera does not take a
continuous moving film, but a very rapid series of still
photographs.

Both camera and projector work on a stop-and-start basis.
The film is not pulled through by the take-up spool, which

indeed is specifically designed so that it does no such thing. It is snatched down by a claw that engages in the sprocket holes at the side of the film. It pauses momentarily while the shutter opens and closes, before moving on again to the next frame. The shutter itself is quite unlike any of those used in still cameras. Normally, though not always, it is a disc with a piece cut out. It revolves between lens and film, so that the light passes through the open sector, and the film moves while the solid part is cutting off the light.

The result, projected in the same way, gives an illusion of natural movement provided – and it is an extremely important proviso – that the rate of exposure (the number of frames per second) is exactly the same on the projector as on the camera. If the camera works more slowly than the projector,

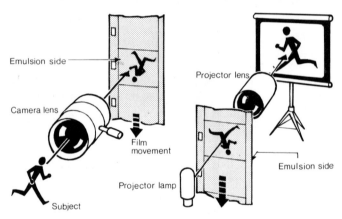

Emulsion side

Projector lens

Camera lens

Film movement

Emulsion side

Projector lamp

Subject

The image formed in a lens is inverted, so the film is run through the projector with the pictures upside down to reproduce normal movement

the image on the screen will move too quickly; conversely if it exposed at a higher rate the movement will be slowed down. This is how 'slow motion' sequences are made. It is also partly the reason why old silent films often look so unnatural on the screen. Modern sound projectors work at higher speeds than the old silent ones, and in addition the older films were taken on cameras that relied for their motive power on the cameraman's turning a handle. Although there must have been a governor in the mechanism, the slightest relaxation of pressure must have produced a variation in the taking speed.

Types of Super 8 camera

The basic Super 8 camera (of which, however, few remain on the market) takes advantage of the depth of field of small-aperture lenses described earlier, to the extent that no focusing is required at all. It has an 'electric eye', which adjusts the aperture so that a constant amount of light arrives at the film, whatever the lighting conditions may be. In addition, there is a warning system to tell you when the light is altogether insufficient. The simplest models were restricted to one speed of film (25/40 ASA), but most allow you to use fast film in difficult circumstances. The electric eye is adjusted automatically when the film cartridge is inserted. So your films should come back to you with reasonably consistent images.

This completely automatic operation leaves you entirely free to concentrate on your shooting, but, not surprisingly, the system is less than perfect. There are two disadvantages: the lack of need to focus means that you cannot focus if you want to, and the automatic exposure control does not allow you to make adjustments for unusual conditions.

The fixed lens will have been set to make the maximum use of the depth of field, probably focused most sharply at about 5 metres (15 feet). Objects nearer than that will become less sharp; they will photograph well enough for most purposes down to about 2½ metres (8 feet) or less on bright days when the lens is closed down further, but closer still they will be noticeably fuzzy. There is nothing that you can do about it unless the makers provide a supplementary lens for close-ups. Similarly, sharpness decreases with greater distance, but more slowly. This is not so important; anything within reasonable range will be sharp enough, and really long shots are never very satisfactory on small-gauge cine, because the film is so tiny that the microscopic images are blurred by the physical properties of the film and the emulsion itself.

Again, to get this sort of depth it is necessary to use quite a small lens aperture, which requires a correspondingly large amount of light. Consequently, you may find that on very dull days subjects closer than 3 metres (10–11 feet) are not quite sharp, although there is plenty of light to see by. Remember that your own eyes adjust themselves to differing light intensities, while the electric eye measures the light in absolute terms.

Automatic exposure

The electric eye is a light-measuring device coupled to the diaphragm, and is perhaps better called a coupled exposure meter; 'electric eye' is simply a colourful advertising phrase.

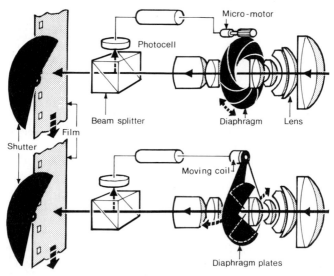

A normal iris diaphragm can be set by a micromotor, but many cameras have a moving-plate exposure control coupled directly to a moving-coil galvanometer

The meter may read through the taking lens or may have a separate little window of its own. In either case, it alters the diaphragm according to the average light falling upon it, over the whole area of your picture and perhaps a little more, on the correct assumption that most subjects are average subjects – street, garden or park scenes. But if there is a great deal of contrast in your view it may produce an exposure that is wrong either for the whole of your picture or for the most interesting part. It would certainly be wrong, for instance, for a shot of fishing nets hanging up with the sky for a background, because it will take into account a vast amount of sky light, whereas what you really want to measure is the light reflected from the nets. The same may happen in any shot where there is a lot of sky – for instance a scene on a beach looking towards the sea. Conversely, if you have a girl in a light dress caught by the sun against a dark wall in shadow, you are likely to get a beautiful shot of a wall with a white blob in front of it.

Nevertheless, your exposure will be right for much the greater part of the time. You simply have to avoid extreme conditions. Colour film is less tolerant of high contrasts than is black and white, because the colours themselves as well as the density are affected by the exposure. It and the built-in meter are most effective in subdued overcast lighting – try filming in the rain, if your lens will take it.

Because of these disadvantages, more advanced cameras are fitted with larger adjustable lenses and exposure controls.

Exposure controls
The simplest exposure gadget is called a backlight control. A backlight switch allows you to double the amount of light that the meter first thought advisable, when you have a lot of sky or other light in the background. This gives you more detail on the darker objects in the foreground, and should cope with your wide-open beach scenes so that you can see the family party clearly. A second position, available on some cameras, halves the light. This lets you get detail in the girl's dress against the dark wall.

Still more elaborate cameras allow you to uncouple the meter and set whatever exposure you please. This facility is used when the conditions are so extreme that the one-stop variation permitted by the backlight control is insufficient. It may be, for instance, that you are peeping in through a window, as suggested in the outline of the vicarage fete film (Chapter 1), or you may want to use an archway to frame a view or a person. In neither case are you interested in the detail of the frame; you want the scene beyond to be perfect

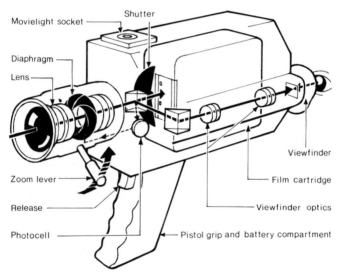

A modern Super 8 camera is normally fitted with a zoom lens and through-the-lens (reflex) viewing. Exposure is controlled automatically by electronic diaphragm control from a built-in photocell

and the frame to be just that – often the blacker the better. In that case you take your camera (or a separate meter) forward until you have a reading of the area where you want full detail. Then you uncouple your meter and set that reading for making the shot. The same might apply to those fishing nets against the sky, though in this case you would be burning out the background in favour of the foreground.

Of course, until comparatively recently, automatic exposure control was a rarity. People made – and continue to make – perfectly good films with the aid of tables or a separate exposure meter (see box below).

Independent exposure meters

Practically all Super 8 cine cameras have integral exposure meters coupled to the lens diaphragm, but in some circumstances (particularly where extremes of contrast are involved: see opposite) better results can be obtained by using separate meters. However, there are often differences between integral and independent meter readings, for three reasons:

● Reflex viewfinders and some zoom lenses absorb light, so their marked stop number may be optimistic. The integral meter allows for this, but the independent meter does not.

● Most independent meters assume that cine film is exposed at $\frac{1}{30}$ second – as was the case with older cameras – but Super 8 cameras with standard shutters tend to expose at $\frac{1}{40}$ to $\frac{1}{50}$ second, and at even less when running at the optimum sound speed of 24 frames per second. On the other hand, XL cameras with the wider-angle shutter do expose at about $\frac{1}{30}$ second. These variations have to be taken into account.

● There may be minor inaccuracies in either or both of the instruments, insignificant in themselves but, compounded by the two factors mentioned above, significant in total.

The solution is to compare readings on each of the instruments in similar circumstances in advance. With my own equipment I find that the independent meter reads one stop smaller than the camera fairly consistently, so that if the meter reads f/11, the camera needs to be set at f/8. This is a fairly reasonable variation, but anyone can check his own instruments in the same way that I have done.

Lenses

The first modification on the lens side is the addition of a focusing mount. The advantages of this arrangement are that you can select the exact setting that brings out your essential point most sharply, and that you can get much closer to your subject. You can have head and shoulder shots or even just heads. You can show details of flowers or carvings, and you can make titles (see page 97) much more easily. Further, since you are not relying entirely on depth of field for your sharpness, you can have large-aperture lenses, which permit you to film in more adverse lighting conditions.

Next is the possibility of varying the focal length of your lens. At one time this was done by physically changing the lens (or by adding supplementary lenses to the standard one), but few Super 8 cameras have interchangeable lenses. Instead, they have 'zoom' lenses, the focal length of which can be varied by pressing a button or moving a lever. The effect of working the zoom is to widen or narrow the camera's eye view. A similar, though not identical, effect can be obtained by moving the camera position farther away from or nearer to the scene, but this is not always possible.

The focal length of a zoom lens is infinitely variable from its minimum to its maximum. You are not, as you would be with interchangeable lenses, limited to a series of exact sizes. Consequently, cameras fitted with zoom lenses almost always have reflex viewfinders. In addition, virtually all have focusing mounts, since the depth of field at the longer settings is insufficient for fixed-focus working to be really practicable.

When using a zoom lens, it is always advisable to focus at the maximum-magnification setting. At this point, the focus is most critical, so it is easier to see when you are right; you are also then safe if you want to zoom in. The focus does not change with the focal length.

A few cameras are now equipped with an electronic automatic focusing system (see box on page 40). Broadly, it is effective where it most needs to be, that is within about 10 metres (30 feet) of the camera and sometimes a little more, provided that there is sufficient contrast in the subject and that the composition contains more or less vertical lines. It will work when someone is walking towards you or away from you, and keep them in focus all the time, but it won't be very effective for a bathing beauty lying on the beach.

As a further refinement, some cameras are equipped with what is called 'macro' focusing. This means that you can get down to within a few inches of a small object, and show it several times life size on the screen.

The zoom lens is an extremely useful feature, both because you have only one lens to carry around and because of its infinite variability. However, like the fully coupled exposure meter it is a fairly new development, and people made perfectly good films before it was available. So it's not indispensable.

Focusing

To focus on a nearby subject, you must know just how much to move the lens control. The simplest system is to measure (or estimate) the distance, and move the focus control until

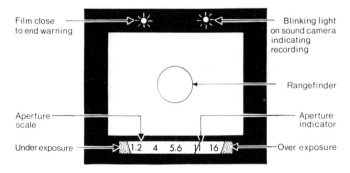

Most viewfinders give information on camera functions, as well as showing the area photographed

that distance is indicated on the focus scale engraved on the lens. With a cine camera, though, you may well want to change the focus during a shot. So it is much more convenient if you can see the focus in the viewfinder. Some cameras have a range of symbols beside the viewfinder image, so that you can see whether you are focused, for example, for a distant scene or for a head-and-shoulders shot.

If you want to be more precise – as you need to be with the longer-focal-length end of a zoom lens – you need a camera with through-the-lens focusing. Most zoom lens cameras have a reflex viewfinder, in which the viewing image is formed by the camera lens (not by a separate set of lenses). In virtually all still reflex cameras, the viewfinder image is formed on a fine etched ('ground glass') screen; so when the viewing image is sharp, the lens is in focus. Many cine cameras, though, form an aerial viewing image. All other things being equal, this is much brighter than a fine-etched-screen image. But it does not show you the focus. Even with fine-etched focusing, because the image is so small and because the depth of field is normally great, it is difficult to

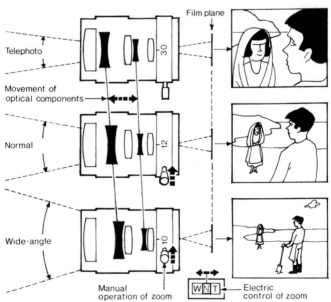

Zoom lenses provide a range of focal lengths to suit the subject

The zoom lens

If you look at the screen of any reflex camera and then place a magnifying glass in front of the lens, you will not be surprised to find that the image on the screen is magnified – though it will be out of focus. If you move the glass nearer to or farther away from the lens, you will get varying magnification. Some lenses use a rather more refined version of this for close-up photography, and a much more refined version is found in the zoom lens.

The zoom lens is contained within one barrel. The sections of the basic lens, placed towards the back of the barrel, are fixed. The magnifying glass is replaced by two or more sections that move in relation to each other up and down the tube, thus producing an image size that can be varied at will according to the specification of the lens (see page 144). This movement affects neither the aperture nor the focusing distance. However, as it alters the depth of field, a slightly misfocused subject can go right out of focus as you zoom from 'wide' to 'tele'.

The production of this type of lens was a great optical achievement. The principle was fairly simple, but the practice a very different matter. The basic problem was that a large number of single lenses needed to be combined to produce the finished article, and their very number produced originally unacceptable losses both in light transmission and in definition of the final image.

More recently, however, new techniques of multiple coatings, which reduce light losses inside the lens, have solved the problem of light transmission. Also a number of new types of glass, each with its own special optical properties, have become available to lens makers, and their use has solved the problem of definition – at least so far as cine work is concerned. (The production of zoom lenses good enough for still work has only just begun.) Thus the modern zoom lens is not only effective for its purpose, but also manageable in size.

Automatic focus

Recently an automatic focusing device has made its appearance on some of the more expensive cameras. The principle is exactly the same as the first optical/mechanical rangefinders, but the movable mirror or prism is worked by a tiny electric motor, which at the same time moves the focusing control of the lens. Electric sensors compare the two images, and stop the motor when the two coincide or, should the main subject be moving, adjust the setting as it approaches or retreats. Such, at least, is the theory, but of course there are snags.

The basic point, as with all automatic devices, is that the camera has no brain. It does not know what you are trying to photograph. Therefore you must be quite sure that you exclude from the picture prominent objects that are irrelevant to your main purpose. This may well mean that, when using the automatic focusing mode, you cannot include foreground frames.

Secondly, one of the best makers point out that their version does not work very well if the contrast is too low, or if the subject is horizontal. Therefore you cannot expect it to do your thinking for you if you are filming a bathing beauty tanned to the gold of the sands on which she is lying, but it will do better if she is standing up against a green background.

The device is less than perfect, and will remain so until someone teaches cameras to think. Used with discretion it can help, but it is much better employed only when action is too quick for hand manipulation, and even then only when there is enough light for the camera to work at a small aperture, and consequently with sufficient depth of field to overcome deficiencies in the focusing.

An auto-focus system is certainly no substitute for true through-the-lens focusing. It is perhaps worthwhile *in addition* to an accurate focusing aid, but do not forego the latter for the charms of auto-focus.

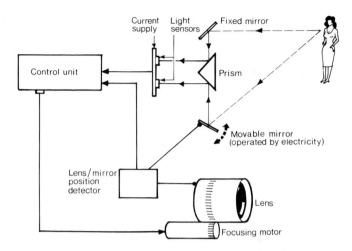

Auto-focus systems keep the lens focused on the subject. Most work by comparing the images from fixed and rotating mirrors. Systems emitting infra-red or ultrasonic pulses are also used

be sure that the adjustment is exact except at long-focal-length settings. This is why it is better to focus at the longest possible setting of a zoom lens, and then move back to the setting you really want.

Most movie cameras, whether with aerial or focusing images, also have a focus-finding device working through the lens. This may work on the split-image principle. In the middle of the viewfinder there is a spot where two images can be seen when the camera is out of focus; to bring it into focus the lens is adjusted until the two images of the object coincide. Sometimes there are two complete images that have to be fused, sometimes there are top and bottom halves that have to be brought together, but in either case the device is easier to use when there is a clear line to look at. If the split is across the picture the line should be vertical, such as a tree trunk or a person; then with a mainly horizontal composition (as for instance in a picture of water lapping on a beach) it is easier to focus with the camera turned on to one side, so that top and bottom become left and right and the rangefinder works across the horizontal line instead of along it. Diagonally-splitting rangefinders are a better solution.

The history of split-image rangefinders is long. The first method, which is used today in many still cameras, works by comparing the view through two mirrors, one fixed and one movable, set as far apart as the construction allows. The

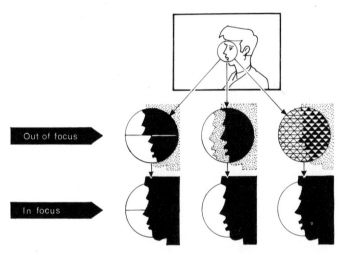

Viewfinder focusing aids are usually one of three types: split image, merging image or microprism

movable mirror is coupled to the lens when the rangefinder is built in. The principle is that of the triangle: if you know the length of the base and the angles at each end of it, you can work out the lengths of the other two sides. To make it easier, the angle produced by the fixed mirror is a right angle, so the only variable is the angle of the moving mirror. It is surprising that it should work so well when the base is measured in centimetres and the other two sides in metres, but it does – thanks to precision engineering.

In through-the-lens viewing (reflex) cameras, the mirror system is replaced by a pair of fixed prisms. These split the out-of-focus image in two optically. There are no moving parts. Quite often the principle is extended: instead of a pair of prisms there are serried ranks of tiny prisms, called microprisms. These split the image up into shards unless it is accurately focused. Even slightly out of focus, the image appears to shimmer. Microprism focusing is especially easy with uneven objects such as trees in full leaf, or shaggy animals; it does not need clear lines or edges.

Choice of focal length

As indicated above, and as we shall discuss in more detail in Chapter 3, the ability to vary focal length enables you to fill your screen with all the picture you want, and nothing but

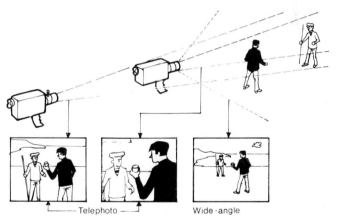

Telephoto   Wide-angle

Choosing the viewpoint alters the relationship between parts of the scene; choosing the focal length determines the area pictured on the film

the picture you want. A short focal length takes in a wide angle of view, and so lets you get the whole of a scene when you cannot go far enough back to use the standard length. Conversely a long focal length gives a narrower view and allows you to concentrate attention on a small piece of the middle or far distance, which otherwise would be lost in a maze of irrelevant images.

A further advantage is that you can deliberately stand back to get your close-up shots. This avoids the well-known effect of your aunt, photographed in a chair, seeming to have enormous knees and a tiny head. That happens because the distance from camera to knees is significantly less than from camera to head. From farther off the difference is less important. This is a good thing even in head-and-shoulders shots – it keeps the nose down to size. Portrait photographers use long-focus lenses for just that reason.

Remember these practical points:

• The longer the focal length, the larger a particular subject will appear in your picture (with the subject the same distance away).

• Conversely, the shorter the focal length, the more of the same view will be included in your picture.

• The longer the focal length, the less depth of field you have available. For instance, a 15 mm lens at an aperture of $f/4$ and a distance of 5 metres will photograph with acceptable definition anything between 2½ metres and infinity, while a 60 mm lens at the same settings will only record satisfactorily from about 4½ to 5½ metres.

Shutters

As we said, the shutter is a revolving disc with a sector cut out. On most cameras the open sector takes up about 170°, and this produces an exposure of ¹⁄₄₀ second or a little less at the usual film speed of 18 frames per second. If you run a sound-on-film camera at 24 frames per second, which can give you better quality, the exposure is around ¹⁄₅₀ second. Some cameras have a shutter that is open for 220°, giving a longer exposure of rather more than ¹⁄₃₀ second, and thus letting more light in. Yet others have a shutter that can be set to either of these two openings.

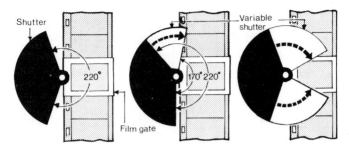

Shutter

Variable shutter

Film gate

In low-light (XL) cameras, the shutter remains open for about 220°, increasing the exposure time. A few cameras offer the choice between normal (170°) and XL (220°) shutter angles, while one or two models have a completely variable shutter, which is excellent for producing fades and dissolves

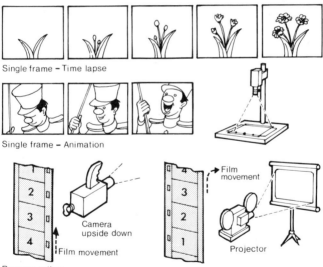

Single frame – Time lapse

Single frame – Animation

Camera upside down
Film movement

Film movement

Projector

Reverse action

Single-frame shooting opens up a range of possibilities, but requires a great deal of patience. To reverse an action, shoot it with the camera upside down and project the film from end to beginning. For projection the film has to be turned round so that the sprocket holes are still on the correct side; the picture is thus reversed left to right

The advantage of the wider opening is that it permits photography when there is too little available light for the narrower one. The narrower, however, is currently in more general use because it produces rather sharper pictures of fast action than does the wider, and because (unless the lens

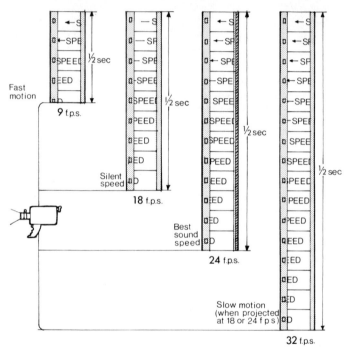

The faster the camera's framing rate, the more frames needed to record an action, and so the slower is the action reproduced on projection

shuts down to a very tiny aperture indeed) the wider may introduce too much light in very bright conditions.

Not strictly a matter of shutters, but affecting exposure length, is the fact that some cameras have variable rates of film movement. Most have a 'slow motion' button, which works the camera at something like double the normal rate, and in this case the exposure is half the normal. Others have a range of speeds, to each of which the exposure is directly proportional. Thus, at 9 frames per second the exposure given by a 170° shutter will be about $\frac{1}{20}$ second.

Some cameras provide what might be called the extreme in slow speeds: they allow you to take one frame at a time. With this, armed with a tripod and patience, you can take, for instance, a sunset sequence one frame every five seconds; the action will be speeded up on projection, but the photography takes an unconscionably long time. Similarly, with longer intervals, you can record the opening of a flower. If you are really keen you can make cartoon films using a series of minutely different drawings, or, more simply, you can make a title appear letter by letter.

The exposure for single-frame work is normally the same as at the standard speed of 18 frames per second, though there are cameras that provide for longer exposures, just as there are some with an interval timer that will cope with your five-second-interval sunset automatically. But these are very expensive models.

Sound

Sound is such a complicated matter that we have a separate chapter on the subject. Suffice it to note here that sound-recording cameras are available; some record on a magnetic stripe on the film itself, others record on an electronically coupled tape.

The more refinements you add to a camera the more you have to rely on yourself to get the settings right, but equally the more versatile they are. Your choice really depends on what you want to do. It is rather like the choice of a car. Some are more accurate, more flexible, more durable and more polished than others. But some are less trouble to operate, and it may well be a disadvantage to have a Rolls Royce if you only want to go shopping locally.

3

Images

Of course you have to know something about how a camera works to get the best out of it, and of course more elaborate and expensive machines have advantages. But the really important thing is the image you produce on the screen. A glance at the results obtained by the classic photographers of the last century, like Julia Margaret Cameron, and at the content and economy of line produced by the classic film directors – Eisenstein, Griffith and the rest – shows what can be done with the most primitive of apparatus, and demonstrates that it is the photographer who makes the picture, not the camera. Designers have given a great deal of help, and cameras can do things impossible a few years ago, but the *photographer* is responsible for what appears on the screen.

Naturally, most Super 8 people are neither able nor prepared to devote the same time and attention to photography as the late Mrs Cameron, and still less have they Eisenstein's opportunities to repeat shots again and again in the search for perfection. Further, in cine photography it is not possible, as it is in still, to use only part of the frame if there are irritating obtrusions. This makes it all the more essential to cultivate an eye for the effective picture, and to get it right first time.

The image you record

When our eyes see something, we select the bit we want to look at and concentrate on it, but the camera records

48

impartially whatever is there. It is vital to remember this, and to watch *everything* in the viewfinder – not just the main subject you want to record.

I am looking out of my window at a plant in a pot, and that is what I see. I do not notice that without moving my eyes I can also take in some empty flower pots, the window frame

Try to see each scene as a well-composed picture, and keep the composition attractive throughout the shot

and the buildings behind. But the *camera* does not know that I am looking at the plant, and the image on the screen will contain all the other things as well. When the film is projected I shall be concentrating on the screen, and I shall have to make an effort to see what the photograph was intended to be about. The same effect is notorious in still photography: Aunt Mary, unfortunately placed, appears to have a palm tree growing out of her hat, and your delightful view of a river valley is reduced to a grey smudge on the horizon between sky and foreground – possibly labelled 'Toilets'. If you are to be satisfied with the results, the image you want must fill the frame.

What could I have done about my plant pot? There are several possibilities, some depending on my equipment. The most obvious was to have moved nearer. Even though I was looking at the plant, I ought to have seen that the other rubbish was coming into the viewfinder, and have moved forward so that it didn't. It pays to get close to your subject.

If I had a zoom lens, I could have used a long-focus setting instead of moving closer physically. This could be a better solution because, as we noticed while talking about lenses (Chapter 2), being too close can sometimes produce a distorted image.

Either method, though, might still leave a problem with the buildings behind. Sometimes you can get round this by changing your viewpoint, so that the pot is against the sky or some other neutral background. Another solution may be to use a long-focus setting, fairly close up, and adjust your focus so that the pot is sharp but the background blurred. This is not always possible, because in bright sunlight your lens aperture will be small, and even at long-focus settings your picture will then be sharp over a considerable distance. One way to get over this is to fit a 'neutral density' filter to the lens. This reduces the amount of light reaching the film, and so requires a bigger aperture (see Chapter 2).

You might think that a fuzzy background would spoil your picture, but this is not necessarily so. It can actually help, if the centre of interest is in the foreground, by avoiding any distraction of your attention.

Since what you do is unalterable, it really is important to know the result you want before you press the button. Some of this you will have considered in your film plan, but sometimes you cannot plan exactly in advance.

A great deal will depend on the actual circumstances when you take your shots, including lighting, colours, and positions available. If you cultivate a 'seeing eye', you will recognise the possibilities of a situation quickly. Large things, for instance, will generally attract more attention than small ones, and bright things more than dull ones. But you can have both circumstances in the same frame, and then you may find that a small bright object leads your eye straight past and beyond a larger dull one. You have to look for the effect, and use it. It's no good fighting facts; it's better to change your position.

Again, moving things catch the eye more quickly than still ones, people more quickly than cars, and – as is notorious in professional filming – children and pets more quickly than adults. The whole thing is pretty logical: for example, if you are filming a public event you have to try to get faces rather than backs. It is easier said than done, in practice. Even well prepared in advance, I have on occasion found myself with photographs of the procession that has just passed – all backs of heads and horses' tails. However, there are a few simple things you can do in intimate filming, such as not photographing the beach cricket match from behind the wicket. Otherwise you will get a large dull back view of the batsman and possibly the wicket keeper, while the rest of the players are dots on the horizon. The great thing to do is to balance your picture so that everything of interest gets attention, and the gasworks do not obtrude.

Balancing your images

Filling your frame satisfactorily is an art in itself. You will have noticed how, of half-a-dozen pictures of the same event at the same time, one catches your eye and outshines all the others. The reason for this is that all the elements were in the right place at the moment of exposure. Volumes have been written on this subject; it is taught as 'composition' in art schools, and rules, or at least guidelines, have been evolved from the study of great painters. The basic thing is to provide stability, balance, and room for movement *into* the picture rather than *out* of it.

For stability, we might think about Van Gogh's *Sunflowers*. A mass of heavy-headed blooms springs from a pot which,

51

whatever it was really like, gives no great impression of weight in the picture. Yet the result is essentially stable, because the painter has shown the edge of the table as a strong blue line, almost connecting with a band round the pot. If you cover that single line, you can see that the picture at once is less satisfactory. Again, if you draw imaginary lines from the outer edges of the table to the top of the highest bloom, you will find that the only two blooms fully outside the triangle are resting, as it were, on the edges of the frame.

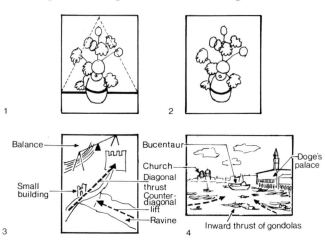

Van Gogh produced a very stable composition for *Sunflowers* (1); simply removing the table-edge almost destroys that stability (2). On the other hand, strong diagonals introduce a dramatic feeling of action, as in El Greco's *Toledo* (3). A range of different angles gives an open, moving effect as in Canaletto's Ascension Day picture of Venice (4)

Now I don't suppose for a moment that Van Gogh thought his picture out in that geometrical, formal way. His painter's eye simply led him to an arrangement that works out like that. But we can learn from him and remember about bases and triangles.

The most dramatic landscape I know is El Greco's *View of Toledo*. Nothing in the picture is movable except the clouds, but the whole scene is alive. The main movement is along a diagonal line from the bottom left-hand corner, along the city wall as it climbs the hill, to the light cloud above the castle on the right. A second line, at right angles to the first, runs from the building in the centre foreground – or rather from a little to the right of it – along the river to the bridge turret and to another building about halfway up on the left. This gives you a cross formed by the long sides of two overlapping triangles – stability again. But more: the cathedral spire flanked by the castle is about one-third down the picture and one-third in from the right, and they are balanced (though in no way dominated) by the bridge turret and building about one-third up and one-third in from the left. These interesting 'third' positions are very strong, and very suitable for leading elements in your picture; also a smaller, more distant object will balance a nearer and larger one in the same way that an ounce weight on a beam will balance a pound on the other end if the pivot is in the right place.

For space and movement, try Canaletto's *Basin of St Mark's on Ascension Day*, with the red and gold *Bucentaur* moored at the Piazzetta, just off-centre. Here the shore line runs right across the picture about one-third up, and is bounded by the Doge's Palace and the Campanile on the right and a domed church on the left. They are well in view, and have space around, though they are not the central items of interest. The excitement and movement is in the crowd of gondolas stretching from the foreground as far back as there is water, and the play of light on the water itself. All the gondolas have room to move (though in some cases not much) and nearly all are moving into the picture, towards the Piazzetta. Although the scene is crowded, nothing of importance is leaving it, to carry your eye outside the picture.

The moving image

Of course these pictures stand still, whereas much of our scene is moving about. Painters are at liberty to rearrange and improve on reality, whereas we are dealing with often obstinate realities of life – where things were built, or grew, and where we can actually stand. But not everything in our film moves, and we nearly always have some choice of viewpoint. The trick is to use the fixed points in a scene to frame and display the real centre of interest. This is something quite different from avoiding irrelevancies: the surroundings of your picture may be very relevant indeed.

When travelling, use your family or companions as a link between places; show them within scenes, but allow the view to be seen as well

Take for instance, your holiday film. People in holiday clothes look much the same all over the world, so you will probably want to show what the place was like and how it was different from other places, as well as to record the presence of your family. If you were in Venice, for example, you could show them between the bobbing gondolas at the Piazzetta and the Doge's Palace – with one prow close up and large, to balance the bulk of the palace. Elsewhere you can place people beneath arches or with trees arching over them.

You may be able to find a place for your carnival shots where the procession enters a square between two impressive buildings, or you can place a shot in Trafalgar Square so that the frame is bounded by a lion on one side and a fountain on the other. Make maximum use of the setting; the thing is to make everything on the screen part of a coherent picture, indeed part of the best picture you can take.

The direction and angle of movement within the screen area can be used both pictorially and for emphasis. Remember the stagecoach in the standard Western tearing away

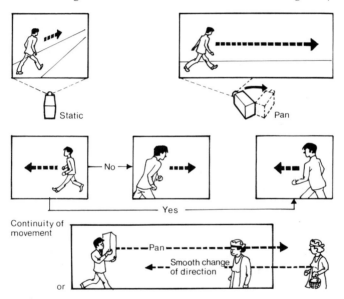

Relate camera movements to the subject. Where there is room, a static camera is best; for cross-movements, pan with the subject. Be careful to avoid confusing the movement by changing viewpoint and direction

from Coffin Gulch? It tends to go between two hills, one a little taller than the other, and to move from one bottom corner of the screen towards the opposite top corner. This gives you action within the frame, with a minimum of camera movement. Moreover, you are pretty certain that the next shot will be round behind the hill, where the other side are preparing a surprise for the coach.

You can use exactly the same principle in your own films. If the people are going away from you, they attract less attention to themselves, but tend to make you expect the camera to follow them – round the Doge's Palace to the Bridge of Sighs, for instance. If they are coming towards you, you rather expect them to do something, or perhaps just to come into close-up for a few moments. You can quiet these expectations by letting the people move off to one side and holding the empty scene for a little. On the other hand you can use them to give continuity and cohesion to your film. Both techniques are valid, but remember that a film is a continuous thing and make use of points like these to hold it together without, if possible, letting it look commonplace. Sometimes you can lead in to a pleasant surprise. Whatever you do, remember that you are making pictures, and the more effective each single frame, the more effective will the film as a whole be.

Varying the image

Shots can be varied in time, distance and angle. The time taken for each shot must vary, of course, with what is going on. With a static shot, try to have the view on the screen long enough to take in the scene, but not so long that you get tired of it. This depends on the scene itself. A long shot of an empty beach has to stay for enough time to imply peace and quiet, but a building may require less time if it is not in itself particularly exciting, or more time if it has fascinating detail. Games on the beach if held too long can begin to look like a cricket team playing for a draw, and if not long enough leave you wondering why the shot was ever made. Any scene is the better for a climax: a caught ball, for instance, in a game sequence.

The great thing is to decide for yourself when the pictorial interest of a scene fades and whether you are tempted to hold a shot simply because it shows little Willie on his third birthday. If you are, don't – or your audience will go to sleep.

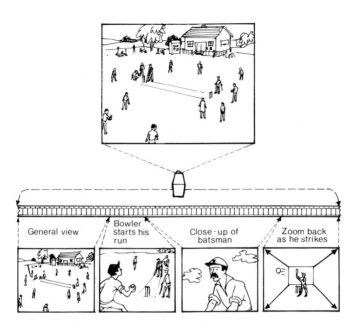

General view

Bowler starts his run

Close-up of batsman

Zoom back as he strikes

In a relatively static situation, add variety to the film by changing angle and viewpoint; avoid panning and zooming except where the action dictates

Take him on several different occasions instead, and made a story out of the shots.

Some shots can be very short, others longer. In the finished film you need a mixture of both to keep the interest going – in the long run your own as well as other people's.

Half closes

When there is a complete shift of interest – to another place, another day, another event – you may wish to mark off one part of your film from the next. Try to make your sequences come to a climax and show, in themselves, when a change is to be expected. To give additional emphasis, or when a sufficiently definite pause signal is not available, the two professional techniques of wiping and fading can be used.

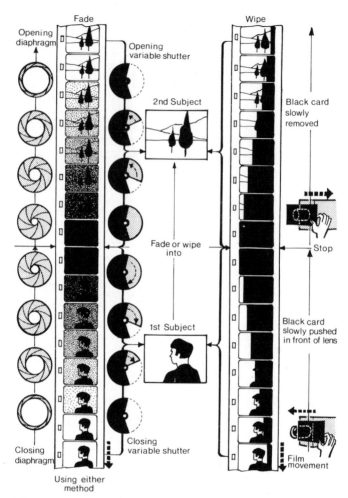

When one scene follows the next in shooting order, you can introduce a variety of changes instead of a simple cut. With the diaphragm or variable shutter the scene can be faded to black, then back into the next scene. Alternatively a piece of card is useful for wipes. In either case the camera must be capable of maintaining the normal exposure, so through-the-lens metering models need manual control

You can wipe your screen clear by passing a piece of cardboard across your lens until it is fully covered, and you can do the opposite by starting with the card there and moving it away. Both are tricky operations unless your camera is on a stand, but much easier if you ask someone else to do it for you. Alternatively, you can swing the camera steadily on to a nearby dark object – a wall, curtain or even the back of someone's jacket. It is essential that whatever you use should be fairly close to the lens, so that the result on the screen is simply a dark neutral shade and does not look like a failed picture.

The fade is theoretically possible to achieve by closing your diaphragm by hand, but often there is still too much light with it closed as far as possible. Try it when the light is not great. Some cameras have fading equipment built into their own mechanism, but these are very definitely in the expensive class. Some even have facilities for 'dissolving', i.e. fading in the second scene while the first is fading out, but this is rare on Super 8 cameras becase it involves winding the film back after the first fade so that the second can be taken on top of it. The cartridge loading system makes winding back difficult.

Angle and distance
It adds interest to your film if you vary the angles and distances of your shots. Take the 'fishing boats leaving' bit of our seaside film. This could include general views of the harbour, medium shots of individual boats, upward-angle shots of masts, downward-angle shots of mooring bollards – perhaps with a rope slipping away – and end with a long shot of sterns and wakes. Some interspersed pictures of fishermen would help too. This may sound a tall order, but you don't need to do it all at the same time, or even in the right sequence; that can be organised later (watch for lighting continuity, though; see page 77). It is always worthwhile bearing in mind this principle of variation, whatever your subject; a close-up of a cheerful face or of a kicked ball can make all the difference to a game sequence.

The same approach is essential if you are to make anything at all of something that obstinately stands still, like a cathedral. The temptation is to move the camera along and round the building, but this is remarkably difficult to do smoothly, and frequently tiring, if not dazzling, to watch.

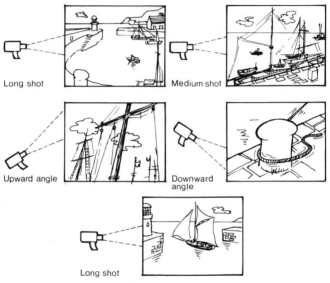

Long shot

Medium shot

Upward angle

Downward angle

Long shot

The more angles and variety in a film, the more exciting it looks

You may have to tilt upwards to show the height of a tower, and doubtless you will want to try a sideways swing ('pan' for panorama); if you do, remember to move slowly and to hold the first and last views for a few seconds, to allow the eye to come to rest. Also try to keep steady, or use a tripod. One trick is to switch to slow motion, which allows you to move firmly and fairly quickly; it is easier than going slowly, and the effect is similar on the screen. But you will probably find that pans are less than satisfactory. Use cutting – changes of distance and angle – instead.

You can start with as complete a view of the cathedral as you can get. This may not be very complete, unless it is more isolated than usual or you can find a high vantage point some distance off. If a fairly complete view is not possible, then perhaps you can get a good shot of the principal facade, which would in any case make a good second shot. You can then go in to a detail shot of the door or a doorway, and cut from that to a perspective view along the side. From this you could turn upwards to show the flying buttresses, with the tower (or spire) beyond them. Interspersed could be detail shots of carvings or gargoyles. If you are allowed to climb the tower, or can find some similarly high point, the roof from above is often of interest.

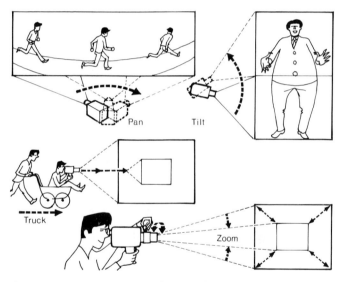

Camera movements can record more of a sequence or add a little extra. Trucking the camera and zooming produce similar but distinctly different effects

Whether you can photograph the interior depends on whether the authorities allow it, as well as on the lighting conditions and the resources of your camera. But most cameras are capable of taking pictures of stained-glass windows lit from without, though the danger here is

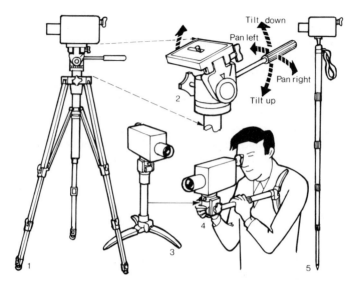

A film camera support is very important for film making. If the camera wavers at all, the picture on the screen appears to float in a disconcerting way. A good strong tripod (1) is the best support; a pan-and-tilt head (2) allows camera movements. When a tripod would be too cumbersome, a small support (3), rifle grip (4) or monopod (5) is a great help

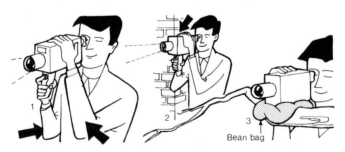

To hold a camera steady, take up a firm stance with both arms braced (1); wherever possible use some extra support (2). A bean bag is good for uneven supports (4)

overexposure and a fuzzy effect round the edges. (Details about tackling interior and problem shots like this can be found in Chapters 4 and 5). If conditions make it possible, you will probably want to take the reredos, the choir screen, and details of carving on the pews and elsewhere. Returning to the outside, you can finish off with another perspective view and a farewell shot of whatever you consider the most striking feature.

The point about using cutting instead of panning is allied to another rule, which is (very broadly) that it is the pictures that are supposed to move, not the camera. You can get a certain amount of movement even in shots of buildings: there will be people moving, or branches of trees or flowers that can be included fairly inconspicuously but effectively. But if you yourself move, you will simply find that your images jump about on the screen. Indeed, it is only too easy to get that effect when you think you are standing still, and it is always better to take advantage of any support that comes handy. You can, for instance, rest your elbows on a low wall or on the back of a bench, or you can press yourself and the camera against a lamp post.

There are numerous devices on the market for holding cameras steady: tripods, unipods, rifle grips and others. To be really effective, though, they need to be fairly heavy and bulky, since a support that vibrates or flexes can be worse than none at all, and to carry them round requires a degree of dedication. Additionally, they are rather conspicuous, and many amateur photographers prefer not to attract attention to themselves, so that passers-by do not turn and stare into the camera. (You can often see this effect in open-air television interviews; there it does not matter very much, but you do not want it on your screen in perpetuity.) On the other hand, these are comparatively minor disadvantages, and though people tend to reserve tripods for specifically photographic outings, there is no doubt that their use produces better and steadier results.

Another way of adding variety is to vary the lighting, though this is possible only within limits. Variations in the exposure of colour film produce variations in colour as well

63

as in intensity, so strong contrasts have to be avoided unless you are deliberately sacrificing one part of your picture for the sake of the rest. Indeed, with the simplest cameras, which have no provision for adjustment of the exposure, it is better to keep the lighting fairly flat – from over one's shoulder in bright sunlight. Where there is a backlight switch you can be more daring, and if you can completely override the automatic meter your resources are correspondingly greater. Lighting, however, is so important that we need to discuss it in detail in the next two chapters.

4

Light

We have touched on lighting conditions in connection with normal-speed and fast film, and mentioned that a filter is usually necessary when using artificial-light film in daylight, and vice versa. The whole question of *why* conversion filters

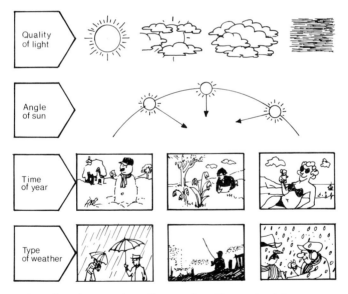

Light makes photographs, still or moving. Choose the right moment for outdoor shots, to give the combination of lighting that you want

are needed must now be considered, as part of the broader subject of the quality of light at the time of exposure and the ways in which film reacts to it. We need to think carefully about this in order to get the best results from our materials.

Daylight itself varies in colour according to the season, the time of day and sky conditions. In addition, the light on our subjects is not only direct, but also reflected from their surroundings, so if the latter have a predominant colour – as do beaches, seas, or large coloured walls – what eventually reaches the film will be tinted accordingly. Now our brains adjust to these changes: unless we think about it, we see the colours that ought to be there, rather than those that really are. We notice the golden glow of a sunset, but often not the tint assumed by a white dress at the same time. We know that snow is white, so we rarely notice that in shadow it often looks blue. Films make no such distinction; they record what is in front of them, in accord with the colour balance with which their makers have endowed them. We can do something to influence what they record, but before discussing that let us define the commoner daylight conditions.

The light from the sky

Broadly, sky conditions can be divided into clear, hazy, cloudy and dull. Some of the effects these conditions have on colour are noted below. But remember, whatever the sky conditions, that the colour composition of the light changes from morning to midday and from midday to sunset.

Morning and evening. Early and late in the day the light of the sun passes through a great deal of dust and haze in the atmosphere, which gives it a reddish or orange tint. It also, of course, casts long shadows. There is nothing wrong with either the tint or the shadows, provided that you want to show that the pictures were taken at that time of day, and that you make due allowance for the shadows in exposure and angle of view. But if you need the shots to cut into scenes made at other times of day, you need to apply some correction.

Sun shining unobscured. When the sun is fully out, colours tend to be very bright and even garish, though some shades look a little washed out. Also, the open expanse of blue sky introduces a faint blue tinge into shadow areas, and there is a lot of ultra-violet radiation, which can in some cases be recorded on your film as blue. Shadows, and therefore contrasts, will be very strong, so you need to be wary about your automatic exposure meter if you want to include much shadow in your frame – some small shadows always give your pictures more substance, of course.

Sun obscured by clouds or light mist. Very light cloud takes the edge off the sun's harshness and reduces the contrast between sunlight and shadow. It also removes the blue cast thrown by open sky, but at the same time the generally sunny effect remains. These are usually rewarding conditions for colour photography, unless, of course, you are trying to depict an atmosphere of extreme brightness or the reverse.

Cloudy bright. There is this to be said for clouds: the more they gather the more even the general lighting becomes, though sometimes they give the light a bluish cast. A bright light filtered through clouds can often be used very effectively, provided that there is sufficient life and colour in the scene before you, and in such conditions you may well find that grass and leaves look beautifully green. Beware, though, of those days when clouds are scudding across the sun. Your automatic meter will take care of the differing quantities of light, but not of the colour changes.

Dull and overcast. Pictures taken under a really dull sky tend to look dull themselves, though the use of a backlight switch to increase the exposure will improve matters. Occasionally, usually when storms are brewing, there is a strange luminosity about, and this can be used effectively, though it can produce problems in consistency within the film. You really need a whole sequence shot before the effect goes. Photographs in the rain sometimes work well: the glint from the water produces highlights of its own, and colours often show up more clearly than you would expect.

Artificial light

It scarcely needs saying that artificial light is not the same colour as daylight. Rooms look different with the curtains drawn and the lights on; when we are choosing cloth for a suit the tailor will usually take the bolts to his door or to a good window to show their true tints. Also, different sorts of artificial light have different effects on colour; ordinary household bulbs give a warm yellow radiance, while fluorescent tubes produce a cold blue-green that is only slightly modified when they are tinted to give a warmer effect.

A third variety of light is produced by photoflood bulbs, which are designed to fit in normal domestic lamp sockets but give a much higher intensity and therefore reduce the exposure needed by the film. The light is slightly more bluish than that from normal domestic bulbs, but still much more orange than daylight. A similar tint is given by the quartz-halogen lamps specifically designed for cine work.

How your film responds to light

Film cannot record 'true' colour in all these varying lighting conditions, but manufacturers compute their emulsions to cope with the commonest ones. The normal film for Super 8 cameras is type A. It is designed basically for photoflood light, and is converted by the filter built in to the camera to record true colour in the middle of a fairly bright day. This filter is in place all the time unless you move it. It must be swung out of the way if you are working in artificial light, or if you are using type G film.

Type G film is the one that works in both daylight and artificial light without a filter in either case. It does this because it is less sensitive to extreme blues and reds than type A, and these are the colours that vary the most between daylight and artificial light. It is a useful compromise at times, but naturally it cannot be expected to reproduce the same range of colours as accurately as type A. The effect on the

68

screen is noticeably different, and this is why it is preferable not to mix the two types on the finished spool.

For similar reasons, a slow Ektachrome type A is available in some regions for mixing with the fast variety, in place of the standard Kodachrome. Again, it is better not to use different makes of material in the same film: if you start with Agfachrome, stick to it right through your film.

Modifying the light with filters

In addition to the built-in filter, other filters can be used for similar purposes – that is, for modifying the colour of light when it is different from the one for which the film was designed. Filters are simply pieces of coloured transparent material that fit on to the front of the lens. They tint the image with their own colour, but in fact they do the opposite of what they seem to do: an amber filter does not add amber light, it suppresses blue. Consequently, most filters call for increases in exposure. This is why normal film is rated at 40 ASA for artificial light and only 25 ASA for daylight: the filter makes the difference. Other filters of all colours are manufactured in a range of shades from dark to light, and each shade is marked to show the increase it needs: for example a 2× filter calls for one stop larger, and a 4× for two.

The change in speed caused by the removal of the conversion filter makes no difference to the operation of cameras with integral meters, because when in position it influences the exposure meter as well as the film. The same is true for additional filters if your meter measures the light coming through the lens. If, however, the meter measures through a separate window – and you can see whether it does by looking at the front of the camera – then you can only use filters requiring an increase of exposure if you have some means of overriding your meter. A backlight control will allow you to use filters requiring double the normal exposure, but for anything else you need a full manual override. Of course, if you can put a little filter on your meter window, that will compensate for the filter on the lens.

Types of filter

Filters are on the market in all the colours of the rainbow and a few others as well. However, we need only concern ourselves with four: amber (also called red), for suppressing blue; blue, for suppressing red and amber; ultra-violet suppressors, which are clear; and neutral-density filters, which do not affect colour but increase the exposure necessary.

Ultra-violet and skylight filters. The colourless ultra-violet filter simply suppresses ultra-violet rays, which are very common in mountain and beach scenes and which if they reach the film turn everything a rather nasty blue. They do not worry the owner of a Super 8 using type A films, because the built-in daylight conversion filter absorbs UV strongly, but they need dealing with if type G film is used, and on older cameras that take type D.

The pale pink or straw-coloured 'skylight' filter also absorbs UV, but in addition it warms up scenes slightly. It is

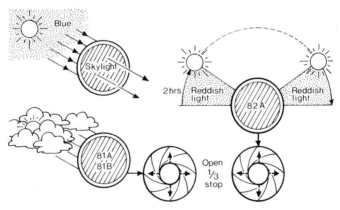

Colour films are designed for white daylight. When the lighting changes, filters are needed to preserve neutral colour balance. The blue of light from the sky or on a cloudy day can be reduced by a pale salmon filter, a 'skylight' or slightly darker 81A or 81B. Early or late in the day an 82A helps remove the rather red colour of the sunlight. All but the palest filters need an exposure increase; the aperture must be altered unless the camera measures exposure through the filter

intended to remove the blue tinge from pictures taken in the sun on bright days. Since, like the plain UV filter, it requires no increase in exposure, and since it has only a small visible effect on pictures taken in other conditions, I leave mine on the lens permanently. It is there when it is needed, and as a bonus it acts as a lens protector.

Blue filters. In early morning and late evening – say two hours after sunrise and two hours before sunset in temperate zones – the light of the sun has a reddish or golden tone. Now this may be exactly the effect you want, and a very good one it is, too. But if you want to get rid of it for any reason – you might want a particular view without traffic, for instance, but with the appearance of full daylight – then the answer is a very pale blue filter. The right sort is technically coded 82A, and is sold as a 'morning and evening' filter. It calls for 1¼ times normal exposure, so the aperture needs to be opened by one-third of a stop. Darker blue filters are available to get rid of even redder tones if you need to do so.

Amber filters. When the blue cast in the light is too great to be overcome by a skylight filter, an amber one is the answer. As noted earlier, there is a lot of blue about on a cloudy day, and sure enough you can buy cloudy-day filters, numbers 81A and 81B. The latter is slightly darker than the former, but both in practice require the same increase in exposure – 1¼ times – as a 'morning and evening' filter does. The same filter may suffice for mountain photography, but for photographing high snow scenes an 81C, needing half a stop more, might be better. Still darker filters are available if needed.

Neutral-density filters. Neutral-density filters make no difference to colour. They simply reduce the amount of light reaching your lens, so that your camera operates at a greater aperture than it otherwise would. We shall go into this a little more fully later, but briefly they are of use when (as may easily happen if you are using fast film) your camera lens will not close down far enough to avoid over-exposure, and also when you want to use a wider aperture so as to have a blurred background to throw up your sharp main subject, as

71

described in Chapter 3. They are available as ND × 2 and ND × 4, opening your lens by one and two stops respectively.

Choosing a filter
Choosing the right strength of filter, and exactly the right colour, for any given light is very difficult by eye alone, partly because of our natural mental adjustment to light conditions and partly because film emulsion does not always react in the same way as the most careful eye. A still photographer can take several shots with different corrections, but this is rarely possible in amateur cine work. However, absolute correction will not be wanted in every case, for the colour of the light adds to the 'atmosphere' of the film. We normally want just to avoid the exaggerated effect that sometimes occurs, and for this purpose a skylight and the palest shades of blue and amber are often sufficient. The skylight is possibly the most useful; you may feel you can wait to get the others until you begin to feel the need for them.

For the meticulous, there exists a gadget called a colour temperature meter, which measures the colour exactly and tells you what filters to use. This is definitely a device for the long in purse, and even if you have one it needs to be used with discretion or your coloration will become monotonous – everything will look the same. Anyone wishing to use such a meter, and indeed to make more than the simplest use of filters generally, should consult the filter manufacturer's literature. Meanwhile, the following table summarises the suggestions made so far for correcting to what might be called 'standard daylight':

Lighting conditions	Filter type	Exposure factor
Red/gold mornings and evenings	Blue 82A ('morning & evening')	1¼
Bright blue sky, especially on beaches and in mountains	Skylight	1
Cloudy bright	Amber 81A	1¼
	Amber 81B	1¼
Mountain snow or other very blue conditions	Amber 81B	1¼
	Amber 81C	1½

Provided that the filters are of high quality, preferably 'multi-coated' to avoid reflections between them, any of these filters can be used in combination with a neutral-density filter.

Choosing the best natural light

The best light for your film depends, naturally, on the effect you want to produce. If you want a film of a sun-drenched holiday, clearly you will look for bright sunlight and be duly cautious about the amount of shadow area in each shot. If you want an atmosphere of mist and drizzle (which, handled skilfully, can be most effective) then, short of highly complicated trickery beyond the scope of this book, you have to wait for the mist and drizzle to appear. And of course there are times when the lighting is forced upon us: the vicarage fete cannot be postponed until the weather is right, nor can the Easter Parade, so we have to do what we can in the prevailing conditions.

However, when a more leisurely approach is possible, my own preference is for a rather hazy or lightly clouded sunlight. There is still plenty of variety in the lighting, and thus life in your pictures, but the contrast is so reduced as to avoid harshness and to allow a much greater range of lighting angles. The latter is, of course, also true on a cloudy-bright day, but here, unless you are striving for a muted effect, you need plenty of colour to make up for the absence of brilliance. It's the 'seeing eye' again.

The position of the sun

In the full blaze of the sun, options are limited by the contrast problem, even given full manual override of the aperture control. Expose for the highlights, and the shadows will be black and devoid of detail; expose for the shadows, and the highlights will be burnt out. Both of these effects, and especially the former, can be used occasionally to produce strongly dramatic pictures, but they become tiring if used to excess. Normally it is better to keep the sun behind and a little to one side of you. Not directly behind, for that produces a very flat effect, and people looking towards the camera are likely to have their faces screwed up. A tiny amount of shadow brings the picture to life.

For much the same reasons, it is preferable to avoid times when the sun is directly overhead, or nearly so. The light has the same flattening effect, and what shadows there are come in odd places: a nose, for instance, may throw a shadow down across the mouth.

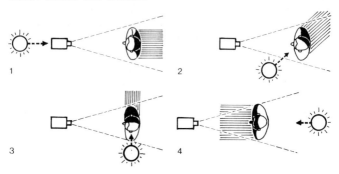

On sunny days the sun's position relative to the subject can make an enormous difference to the way a subject is recorded on the film.

The same basic position, with the sun at about 45° to one side and between 45° and 70° up, is naturally valid in conditions of diffused light, but you can also be more adventurous, and go in for what is called 'modelling'. This term is used in photography to describe the use of light to show the full shape of solid objects. To achieve this, you make use of shade as well as light – the *chiaroscuro* of painters.

Even on the dullest days every object has its lighter and darker sides, as you can see by walking round, say, an ornamental urn in a garden. If you look at it with the light directly behind you so that you can only see the light side, you will find that its shape and the details of its design do not stand out very well. Indeed, if you photograph a ball and a disc from this position you won't see much difference in the results.

74

However, if you move to one side you will see that the cast shadows, light though they may be, pick out the details of shape and design, and the effect is more pleasing to the eye and the camera. The 45° angle achieves this: a greater angle is only suitable for specialist figure shots, but can be adopted to show up the texture of, say, a stone or roughcast wall. With colour film this effect cannot be used to excess, but with discretion it can add liveliness to the pictures, and varying the angles will give variety to the film.

Naturally, none of the foregoing is intended to rule out photography in the morning and evening, when the sun is low in the sky. Providing that due allowance is made for the long shadows, the results are most pleasing, although this time of day is best reserved for special morning or evening sequences: even with correcting filters such shots will look different from full daylight ones and will not mix very well.

Problem shots

In the section in Chapter 2 on exposure controls, we noticed that there were occasions (such as the vicarage fete shot of the inside of a room taken from the outside) when an automatic control is likely to give you the wrong exposure for the part of the picture you really want to see. Sometimes you can get over this by using your backlight control and thus doubling the exposure, but more often you will need more than a one-stop increase. This can only be done by taking a reading from the area of maximum interest, whether by getting really close or by zooming in, and then setting that exposure manually, with the meter uncoupled.

Of course if you can keep the frame out of your viewfinder altogether, or nearly so, this problem is solved. There is still another, however. The light from a window is very highly directional, and also falls off rapidly as you get farther into the room. I have just taken a series of readings from the palm of my hand, and from a light wall in a room with a very large window. My hand, close to the window and facing the full light, requires f/11 with a fast film, but with the back of my hand to the light the palm needs *f*/5.6. The wall one metre (three feet) from the window needs *f*/8, but needs *f*/5.6 at two metres and very shortly begins to need *f*/4 and even more. Thus any window-lit shots taken, whether from inside or outside, need to be grouped close together so as to reduce the variation. They also benefit if a reflector such as a white sheet, a projection screen or some matt aluminium – as described in Chapter 5 – is placed on the dark side to lighten up the shadows.

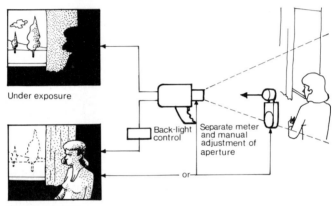

Exposure meters, hand-held or in the camera, are calibrated for normal scenes. With a bright background, foreground subjects are underexposed. The backlight control can correct this, as can manual-exposure cameras set for the foreground

An extreme example of this type of lighting occurs in the case of a stained-glass window, taken from the inside. This is a difficult shot to get right, and impossible if the sun is shining directly on the window. Since the general interior is likely to be on the dark side, if not very dark, you will not be able to get any detail on the inside of the frame at the same time as a proper rendering of the stained glass. No general meter reading will cope with this situation: you can only get the right exposure if you take your camera so close to the window that none of the surrounding dark area is visible. If you can't do this, try taking a reading outside the building and doubling it for your shot. It might come off, though much would depend on the density of the staining.

Another reason for keeping your exposure as low as possible in these circumstances, or indeed whenever a window appears in an interior shot, is the phenomenon known as *halation*. When a very bright area appears in the frame next to a very dark one, the bright light tends to spill over into the dark area (actually by reflection from the back surface of the film material) and causes haloes to form. These haloes make small divisions in the window, such as the lead in leaded lights, disappear completely, and also confuse the general outline. So the rule is to keep to the minimum exposure.

These difficulties are akin to those of shadows in bright sunlight, where again one can only expose for the highlights and let the shadows black themselves out; this is basically what happens when you use an automatic meter.

Mixed light
The effect of artificial light is dealt with more fully in Chapter 5, but it is as well to mention here that any temptation to switch on the room lights inside the vicarage window should be resisted. Natural and artificial light will not mix, except with special precautions – and even then they do not mix well. Without precautions you will get a surprising and unpleasing variety of colours.

Lighting continuity

The fact that the colour of daylight varies so much needs to be taken into account in planning the shooting of your sequences. If a series of actions is supposed to be taking place at roughly the same time on the same day, they all need similar lighting. To take an extreme example, it would look very odd if some shots were taken in bright sun and some under a thundercloud, and it does show if the sun's angle changes considerably between shots. The ideal is to take all the shots for a sequence on the same occasion, but if this is not possible then take a note of the time and lighting conditions of the first set, and make the remainder of the shots in as nearly the same conditions as you can.

Similar conditions may apply to a whole film. For instance, if you are making a story film and the story is contained within a single day, the lighting and weather conditions throughout the shooting must be basically similar. There can be violent variations of weather in the same day, of course, but unless they are part of the story it is better not to strain your audience's credulity. However, in many films consistency from beginning to end is not so important, particularly if the sequences are quite clearly intended to record separate occasions, such as the run up to the vicarage fete or the different stages of a journey. But each sequence must be consistent within itself.

Similarly, when you are using artificial lighting, you must take care that each part of a sequence has compatible lighting. It is of the utmost importance that lighting, whether natural or artificial, should not vary drastically in direction or strength within the space of a scene only minutes long. Light is a wonderful tool if you use it with care, but it can betray you if it is not handled properly.

5

Low light and artificial light

There are times when you want to photograph what your meter tells you is impossible. Sometimes the meter is telling the truth, but there are occasions when, either with an ordinary camera or with a more advanced model, you *can* produce the effect you want.

The simplest is an evening scene at a fair, with coloured lights and so on all around. Your meter will undoubtedly sneer at you, because it is taking an average reading including all the black bits. But the shot is worth trying: your camera will be at its widest aperture, and may well record the lights even though nothing else is visible. You can only try – sometimes it will work and sometimes it won't.

Then there is the occasion when you want an evening or night scene to round off a film, with some detail showing. Your meter will be quite right in saying 'no', but if you can override the automatic meter you can, with some practice, produce a similar effect. You make your film in the evening, when the light is beginning to fade but is still sufficient to give you a reading, and expose at two or three stops less than the reading tells you. For preference you should take the reading with your back or side to the light, but make your exposure facing the other way, so that you are photo-graphing the dark side of the scene. Unfortunately the one-stop reduction given by a 'bright foreground' backlight control is unlikely to be enough, but if that is all you have, you can try. In any case, you will have to experiment a bit to get the effect you want, and you might find a blue filter useful. It is advisable to use a lens hood, to prevent stray light from reflecting on the lens surfaces and producing unwanted spots.

This, though, is not really low-light photography; it is a way of producing a special effect in normal conditions. Filming when the light is genuinely poor, which includes working indoors on quite bright days and all but very highly specialised artificial-light work, needs special preparation, and is practicable only with the right equipment (preferably an XL camera, described later).

Film speed

The right equipment includes fast film, which requires only a quarter of the amount of light needed by normal film. This obviously entails an adjustment to the coupling between meter and lens. Where the adjustment is possible, it is made when you put the cartridge into the camera. Or, to be exact, it is not made. When you put a normal-speed cartridge into the camera, it works a little switch that turns the meter over to the slow speed. The fast-film cartridge is so made that it does not touch this switch. Most cameras have this control, but obviously you need to be certain that yours has before you start.

You may wonder why we have two film speeds instead of using the fast one all the time. The less important reason is that fast film is not as good as the normal sort. Although its quality is perfectly acceptable, it has poorer resolution – that is to say it does not give quite as sharp an image on the screen. The extent to which this matters depends to a great extent on the size of the screen you propose to use: the larger it is the more obviously less sharp the picture.

The chief reason is that fast film is actually too fast for the camera in bright daylight. The lens cannot be shut down far enough to get the exposure right, and because of the already tiny hole it is not possible to manufacture a lens that can be without losing too much definition. Some low-light cameras have a neutral-density filter in the diaphragm mechanism; this allows the light to be reduced enough even in bright sun.

Without that facility you are likely to get an overexposed image, thin and of poor quality and colour rendering. You can get over this by fitting your own ND filter, but you are still left with the slightly poorer performance of fast film.

Low-light cameras

Many cameras are specially equipped for photography in poor light. They frequently have 'XL' (for the rather odd phrase Existing Light) included in the manufacturer's model number. Their characteristics are usually that they have a lens of f/1.2 maximum aperture instead of f/1.9 or less (i.e. about one stop larger than the largest otherwise fitted) and they have the wide-angle 220° shutter mentioned in Chapter 2 or, in the more expensive outfits, a shutter that can be set at either 170° or 220°.

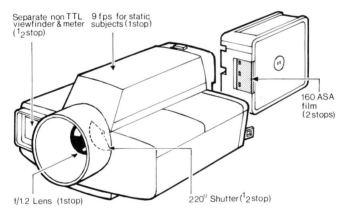

Separate non TTL viewfinder & meter ($\frac{1}{2}$ stop)

9 fps for static subjects (1 stop)

160 ASA film (2 stops)

f/1.2 Lens (1 stop)

220° Shutter ($\frac{1}{2}$ stop)

Kodak introduced low-light Super 8 movies with their XL cameras. They could take pictures with one-sixteenth (four stops less) of the light needed by a normal camera and film combination, or one-thirtysecond for static subjects by reducing the framing rate. Newer designs have zoom lenses, reflex-viewing TTL metering and other refinements

A further refinement of the shutter is the facility to close the opening completely while shooting, or to open it from the closed to the operating position, thus producing the fades mentioned earlier. In theory it is possible to produce a variant of this whereby the shutter opening could be set at a number of prearranged angles to give proportionately lower exposures when necessary, thus avoiding the over-exposure problem in bright light. However, that complicates not only the shutter mechanism but also the meter coupling, so variable-angle shutters are almost unknown on Super 8 cameras.

Some cameras provide for exposure at 9 frames per second instead of the usual 18 or 24. This doubles the exposure time for very adverse circumstances, but is only useful for scenes without movement. Since the film will be projected at double the taking speed, any movement will appear to be twice as fast as it really was. While this might be good for a laugh occasionally, it would not help to convey the atmosphere inside a cathedral.

Naturally, all these modifications are expensive. Even the bare addition of a 220° shutter to a standard camera means that the film has to be moved more quickly between frames, and so involves more delicate and complicated machinery than is really needed for standard use. But if you have the refinements – or some of them – you really can film in many circumstances that would defeat you without them. You can hope to record comparatively dim interiors, you can shoot at dusk and (within limits) in brightly lit streets or floodlit areas at night, and night interior shots will need much less artificial lighting. In all these conditions, though, your focusing needs watching carefully. An $f/1.2$ lens working at full aperture has little depth of field for nearby shots even when set at around normal focal length; you will often need to zoom to a narrower angle than this to get effective results, so reducing the depth of field still further.

Artificial light
Street lights and floodlights are, of course, forms of artificial light. Moreover, they are the only forms of artificial light

likely to be available to us in the open. No portable light source will carry far enough to be effective for photographic purposes, except perhaps for small groups in a private garden. But with care the existing light will be sufficient for low-light cameras. The really dark bits won't come out at all, of course, so the shots need to be directed at the bright sections – and of course the meter will show as soon as you move your viewfinder to an impracticable area.

Even so, to get the best results, you have to examine very carefully which areas really are illuminated. The lighting in a shop window, for instance, is designed to show off the goods on display, not to light the street outside; floodlighting is designed to show the building, sports ground or whatever at which it is directed, and the spillage on to other things is negligible. A shop window one metre (three feet) off the ground will throw very little light on a dry pavement, at least in photographic terms, though it may show up someone staring intently into it at close range.

Reflecting surfaces help considerably: wet pavements may well show up and help to light other things, as may a lake, a pond or even a puddle. You can get remarkably interesting results by using them, and a few experiments will quickly show you what is and what is not likely to make an attractive shot.

Interior scenes
Interior scenes lit by artificial light are in a way easier than outdoor ones, because you are likely to have more control over the lighting – except, of course, on public occasions. In another way they are more difficult, because you have to organise your own lighting, and lighting is an art in itself.

The basic difficulty is that artificial light is very much more uneven than you are inclined to think it is. Eyes adjust very rapidly to changed light and so convey a false impression to the brain, and we rarely remember about the inverse square law we were taught at school. This states that the intensity of light drops according to the square of the distance from the light source. Thus if we call the light intensity at one metre (three feet) from the source one unit, at two metres it will be one-quarter, at three one-ninth, at four one-sixteenth and at five one-twenty-fifth. In camera terms this means that if *f*/11 is the right stop for an object at one metre, then at two it will be *f*/5.6, at three about *f*/4, at four *f*/2.8 and at five *f*/2 or thereabouts. Every time you double the distance between lamp and subject you need to open up by two stops. This will be taken care of by your automatic metering if you have a bright enough light – it has to be very bright indeed – and you photograph something moving towards or away from the lamp. It will be all right, that is, so long as your meter is taking only your subject into account, and not the darker areas behind it.

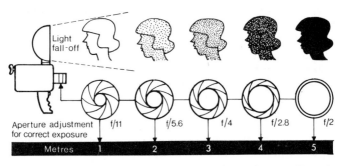

Light from a movielight on the camera reduces dramatically with distance. To compensate, shoot through a wider aperture for distant subjects

The rule applies to all lighting, even, in theory, daylight. The sun is so far away that for practical purposes it is the same distance from everything in the open, but inside a room the window is just as much a light source as a lamp, which is why we got the rapidly falling meter readings described in Chapter 4.

'XL' cameras are designed to function effectively in ordinary domestic lighting, and so, within limits, they will. But given the rapid reduction in effective light as you move away from the source, and given also the average arrangement of domestic lighting, the results are bound to be patchy. Most rooms have a central ceiling light, or perhaps two, backed up by one or two standard or table lamps in strategic places, or alternatively a few wall lights. They all have shades on them to reduce the direct glare. The result is that you have pools of light on the floor under the lamps, and the light in the rest of the room falls off both because of distance and because of the shades. The unlighted corners of the room are always pretty dark from the camera's eye view. Not only will the lighting on your subjects be very varied, but the variaton can be complicated by the areas behind the subjects themselves, if you are using your automatic exposure setting. You will get a record, then, but if you 'follow' your subjects with the camera the background light-level changes will change the exposure, which may look odd. In general, in domestic lighting you should position your subjects with care, so that they look well lit. Then apply the old rule: it is your subjects that should move, not your camera.

Supplementary lighting for non-XL cameras

Interior work is not restricted to low-light cameras, but with the standard types you need to provide about twice as much light by means of supplementary lighting.

The simplest way of increasing the light is to add a 'movelight' to your camera. This is a gadget that fits on to the camera itself and, being connected to the main power supply, directs a stream of highly concentrated illumination on to your subject. It is akin to a flash fitted to a still camera, and has similar advantages and disadvantages. When no other arrangement is possible or convenient it will get you a picture, but one with the usual staring eyeballs and hard shadows inevitable when the light comes directly from the camera position. It has the further disadvantage that, if used for more than a very few minutes, the lamp can get dangerously hot.

The light intensity from a movelight falls off with distance, just as it does from any other source, and indeed the effect is compounded because the light moves with the camera: the farther off your subject is, the less light it gets, so you can't expect a range of subjects at different distances all to be properly exposed. You should try to keep the things you are interested in at much the same distance away, preferably near the background. Also, when using the automatic exposure setting, avoid large dark patches and also large objects nearer than the main ones; both would affect the exposure reading.

One way of reducing both the direct glare and, to some extent, the problem of distance is to tilt the movelight upwards so that the light is reflected from the ceiling instead of shining directly on the subject. Naturally, this also reduces

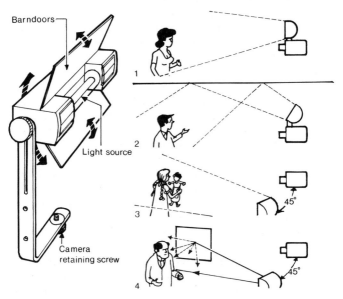

Movielights often use tubular tungsten-halogen bulbs. Barndoors allow the lit area to be adjusted to suit the subject. Direct light is simple but not particularly attractive (1). Bouncing the light from a white ceiling gives a softer and more even illumination (2). To provide natural-looking modelling, move the light away to one side (3). This can produce dark shadow areas; a white reflector is the best way to lighten them (4)

the intensity very considerably, but it avoids harshness and produces a much more even light. You may have seen still photographers doing the same thing with flash, for the same reason. The results tend to be more pleasing, though frequently the complete diffusion of the light produces a rather flat effect.

Flood lighting

When time and facilities are available, for instance in your own home, you can produce much more artistic results by using studio-type lighting.

There is no need to buy special equipment for this, although naturally you may want to do so if interior work becomes a major interest. You need nothing but a few photoflood bulbs and perhaps a spot-type bulb with an internal reflector, all obtainable at any good photographic shop. They will fit into ordinary light sockets.

The high light intensity is produced simply by using thinner filaments than normal for the main supply voltage. (If you fitted a 230-volt photoflood into a 120-volt socket, it would seem rather like a normal lamp, though perhaps not so bright.) Because of this, the bulbs have a short working life – nominally about two hours – but since they are only used for short periods at any one time, they often last much longer, with ordinary care, than that suggests. To conserve them, some photographers make up special switching arrangements: while the scene is being set up the lamps are coupled in pairs, in series, so that they work on half voltage, and are only switched to full voltage while filming is actually taking place. This is quite simple if the bulbs are housed in table or standard lamps, but obviously impossible if they are to be in ceiling or wall fixtures. But even without such arrangements, they seem to go on for quite a long time providing they are allowed to cool down before they are moved.

The advantage of mobile lighting is that it can be placed where it is wanted – near the subject – instead of on the camera, where it isn't. But it can still produce hard shadows and, with several lights, a confusion of cross-lighting. Shades that shield the camera from direct rays are an advantage, but because of the high temperatures they need to be well ventilated and not of delicate material.

The whole scene needs to be studied with care before any shooting; place the lamps so as to avoid harsh contrasts and, if there is to be movement, changes in lighting from one part of the room to another. This can be achieved using existing household fittings, but naturally it is easier if you have ones designed for the purpose. Floodlamp holders usually have metal shades shaped roughly like half an egg and have a matt aluminium finish inside, to provide as nearly as possible an even distribution of light directed to the place where it is

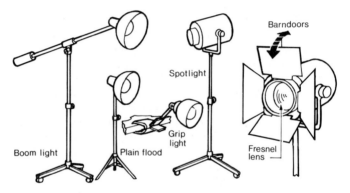

Lighting equipment makes indoor filming much easier. Photolamp 3400 K (Photoflood) bulbs or their tungsten-halogen equivalents are the best choice for Super 8. (Neither photolamps nor photofloods need special housings)

wanted. They can have short stands, which need supporting by a table or a shelf, or tall ones that stand on the floor. The latter often have a more sophisticated arrangement for adjusting the precise direction and angle of the light than the common simple swivel. They sometimes have a swan neck, and sometimes a counterbalanced boom that allows considerable adjustment of height as well as of angle.

Spotlights are designed, obviously, to pick out or emphasise areas of special interest. A proper spotlight has a lens and mirror, rather as a projector does, and is capable of being adjusted to give a wider or narrower beam as required. The spot-type bulb mentioned before cannot, of course, be adjusted, but if you have a sufficiently flexible method of mounting it – a spring clip with a swivel will do wonders attached to a book case or a pair of steps – you can control the beam fairly well with a piece of cardboard with a hole in the middle mounted in front of it. The farther away from the bulb the hole is placed, the more selective the beam will be.

Another aid to indoor (as well as outdoor) lighting is the use of reflectors. Their purpose is to lighten the dark side of a subject so as to reduce excessive contrast without destroying the modelling and the reproduction of texture given by illumination from the side. Any pale surface will help to do this, but white or matt aluminium are best: a pronounced tint in the reflector will also tint the subject, as I realised too late after working in a pink-walled room. White or cream walls are suitable, and so are white paper or sheets. Mirrors are no use; they reflect too harshly and produce a directional effect, which it is better to avoid. Crumpled aluminium foil is useful, but even better is the sort of matt aluminium sheet sold these days for lying on to sunbathe. Even your projection screen can be pressed into use.

Where to put the lights

In discussing lighting angles for daylight work, we saw earlier that probably the best general-purpose position of the sun was at about 45° to the camera's shooting line. Reasonably enough, a similar arrangement is a good starting point for indoor lighting. Try placing the principal flood (which, incidentally, could be a movelight if you have one) rather above the camera level and well off to one side. The precise angle can be found by experiment, by moving the light until you get the effect you want. It will depend, naturally, upon the subject, but 45° is a good average position if you are photographing people.

This single flood, though, will light only about three-quarters of the face in front of your camera, leaving the rest in comparative darkness; there is no natural diffusion to relieve the shadow, as there is in the open. So we need something to supply this deficiency. Try a reflector on the dark side, and perhaps a domestic table lamp as well. This is sometimes adequate. Watch, however, for the deep black shadow thrown by the main light, and keep it out of the picture so far as possible, because it looks unnatural.

Another way of lightening the shady side is to use a second, smaller flood slightly below camera level and either in line with it or a little to the side away from the main light. The comparative strengths of the two can be adjusted by moving them towards or away from the subject until the effect looks right. A reflector can be used at the same time.

To these two lights can be added a spot, to stress a point of particular interest or perhaps just to light up the subject's hair. But this introduces a note of staginess, and is almost worse than useless if the subject is going to move about much, for the spot would need to follow. This would be quite appropriate if you were shooting a dance routine or something similar, but it needs a good assistant to aim the light.

More than one lamp means more than one shadow, which looks highly unnatural and should be avoided if possible. Sometimes you can avoid unwanted shadows by a careful choice of camera viewpoint, but usually more is needed. If the subject itself is light-coloured, and if the background colour is immaterial, a matt black sheet behind and fairly well away from the subject would modify the effect. If, however, as is very likely, there is nothing suitable handy and if, as is even more likely, you want to show that your subject is in a room and not a funeral parlour, try lighting the background itself. The lamp used for this purpose should preferably be behind the subject – but out of the camera's view, of course. It can often be masked by a table, or by the subject's chair, or any other solid object that forms part of the scene. It must be fully masked, however, so that odd streaks of light do not creep under the chair to make an unexplained pattern in front of it.

Movement round the room
So far we have assumed that the subject, though doing something (painting, knitting, or playing with a toy), is more

Movement is the essence of films. Pan with a moving subject to keep it still in the frame, and the background appears to rush past (Ed Buziak)

Overleaf: A movielight offers bright lighting indoors. On top of the camera, though, it provides little modelling and throws harsh shadows and a 'hot spot' on the wall behind. For better results, move the light away to one side and use a reflector or a second light to lighten the shadows. With a wider-angle shot, lighting is even more difficult. A single light well to one side of the camera makes a feature of the shadows. If you don't want this, softening them really is not enough; too much fill-in produces two shadows, which is even stranger. A compromise, with the light closer to the camera, is often more natural

Opposite, top: Modern XL cameras and film can be used practically anywhere. Children in the bath are excellent subjects, and a tub sequence is a great addition to any family film (Ed Buziak)

Opposite, bottom: When travelling, take shots from vehicles. They are ideal continuity between action sequences – and special forms of transport such as San Francisco cable cars are fascinating in themselves. Filming from a moving vehicle causes problems, but slight joggling of the camera may be acceptable in brief shots

Above: Massed animals are always in motion. When they are in the distance and need the long focal length ('tele') setting of a zoom lens, the camera has to be firmly supported to ensure that the rocks don't move!

Opposite: It is seldom possible to record a scene like this continuously from start to finish – indeed the result would be far from ideal. Cut from shot to shot to indicate the progress of the action (Michael Barrington Martin)

Opposite, top: When making fiction films it is often possible to set the scene with a general shot, then confine the action to close-ups against appropriate backgrounds that could match the scene

Opposite, bottom: A low-angle shot from even a familiar place such as New York's Central Park can produce a weird, almost ruined, setting suitable for a fantasy film

Above: The simple narrative film ends on a suitably romantic note (Michael Barrington Martin)

Overleaf, top: Sunsets are obvious ends to films of any sort. Try to make them appear part of the action, though (Michael Barrington Martin)

Overleaf, bottom: Often a seaside or nautical film is better finished with a brightly lit and active seascape

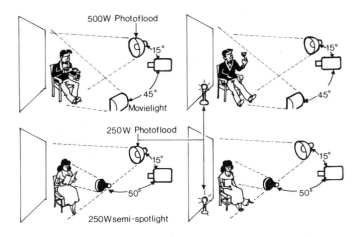

For most scenes the main (key) light should be the only one to cast visible shadows. A second, less bright, light lightens the shadows without confusing the picture. For overall and background lighting, a bare Photoflood bulb is ideal

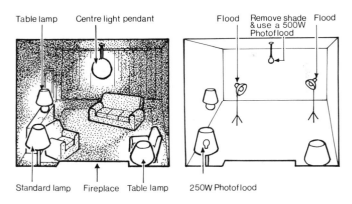

Normal domestic lighting is not very bright and is very uneven. To provide brighter and better-distributed light, replace the ordinary bulbs with Photofloods, and use one or two supplementary flood-lights

or less static. Movement round the room introduces more complications, both of lighting and of focusing.

Because of the rate at which the intensity of light decreases with distance, lamps set up to illuminate a table and chair won't be adequate to cover someone coming in at the door and sitting down at the table. Such a shot will need one or more additional lights to cover the whole area to be photographed, and more background lighting so that your subject doesn't change shadows while moving. The main lights have to be set up in a line parallel to the movement, to make the illumination more or less constant for the whole shot.

The difficulty about focusing is that you are bound to be working at or near the maximum lens aperture and at long focal length, when depth of field is least, so any appreciable movement towards or away from the camera would call for instantaneous adjustment. The effect should be minimised by using the widest-angle setting of the lens, so that you have the maximum possible depth, but even that depth won't be much. An automatic focus control would be a real help here, but failing that the only practical step you can take is to arrange for the movement to be *across* the camera's field of view, and thus in the same plane of focus, instead of towards or away from the camera.

Other light sources
We have not considered the very common and often very bright fluorescent lighting, which, particularly in its 'daylight' version, looks as if it ought to be suitable for general lighting, particularly since it throws no definite shadows. Unfortunately, this is not so. Most lighting is a mixture of the colours of the rainbow (the visible-light spectrum); daylight has them all, often with a slight preponderance of blue and sometimes of red, while tungsten lights (domestic and photoflood lamps) are deficient in blue and strong in oranges and reds, but still contain all the colours in between. In contrast, fluorescent lights have bits from various parts of the spectrum but miss others. To complicate matters still further, different tubes have different colour make-ups, and only the

92

manufacturers can tell you what they are. Consequently, the effect of known tubes is very difficult to balance for colour photography, and of unknown tubes even worse.

There is a filter (coded FL-A) that is supposed to work with 'daylight' tubes, and some 'warm white' tubes can be used without a filter. Type G film minimises the oddity. Even then, the effect is only barely predictable and can be odd in the extreme, so it is better to avoid fluorescent light if at all possible. The same is true of sodium lights – the yellow-orange ones common in road lighting – except that there is no filter that is effective within their glow.

Mixed light

As mentioned briefly at the end of Chapter 4, it is inadvisable to back up daylight with artificial light in the dark spots, because the colours they produce are so different. Broadly, the same warning applies to allowing daylight to creep in to your artificial-light shots.

However, there are two ways in which, if really driven to it, you can combine the two. One is to cover the windows with orange plastic sheet and expose as for artificial light. The other is to mask your floods and spots with blue filters and expose for daylight. Both these methods involve a considerable reduction in the effectiveness of the light sources, the blue system more than the orange. You can, in fact, buy blue filters and orange plastic sheeting of the right specification, but unless you do your light still will not be right, and in fact could be right out. Consequently, it is preferable to use one or other light sources and not try to mix the two.

Practice and the seeing eye

In writing it is only possible to give the most general guide to artificial lighting. Once again, you have to look at the whole scene with great care, not only the bits that you want to photograph but also the bits you can't help photographing because they are there. The whole scene needs to be studied with care before any shooting, and the lamps placed so as to avoid harsh contrasts and violent changes of illumination.

The object is usually to make the finished film look as natural as possible. If by any chance it is supposed to look unnatural or spooky, it must still be consistent within itself. In this, as in most things, a few experiments will be valuable – and practice makes perfect.

In filming, light is your pencil and paintbox. You cannot, in colour, make such a dramatic use of light as you can in black and white, but you can still use light and shade. While the forceful use of colour is important, you can show up your colours and your subjects better by making all possible use of lighting and camera angles. Flat lighting is safe, but much less effective than the controlled use of modelling, in daylight as well as indoors. The more interesting your lighting, the more interesting your film.

6

Perfecting the outline

A film, whether sound or silent, should explain itself in visual terms. We are dealing primarily with pictures, not words. A great deal of explanatory material will be filmed 'on location', so to speak, but some can be (perhaps has to be) filmed afterwards. There are three aspects to this self-explanation, known as continuity, link shots, and titling.

Continuity

Having continuity simply means making sure that your audience are not puzzled by anything in the sequence of shots. Makers of feature films go to extreme lengths to make sure that the decor and costume of each shot match the last one. They have to, since two shots supposedly continuous may be taken months apart. There is no need to be so meticulous in casual productions. No-one is going to suppose that you visited Hyde Park, Greenwich Museum, Hampstead Heath and the Tower of London all on the same day, so costume doesn't matter much. But if the visits are supposed to take place during the same week or fortnight, you should avoid fur coats in one scene and open necks in the next. More important, you don't want the same girl in three different bikinis in what purports to be the same beach sequence. Apart from anything else, it could provoke unseemly questions about what has been going on.

Films that aim to compress the action (*A Day in the Life of . . .*) into a recognisable shape are different. Here there is a purpose in keeping some consistency of dress and style, so as not to distract attention from the main point – what the subject looked like and did at that particular time. Films that tell a specific story are different again: the actors are subordinate to the story, so they must be consistent, just as in a feature film.

Continuity as a link
Another form of continuity is achieved by the type of sequence-planning we proposed for the fishing-harbour scene. If you show a boat outside a harbour, then the harbour itself and finally the boat alongside, the sequence is jerky, and there is no special reason to assume that the two boats are the same. If you put in the shots of bows, heaving line, mooring cable and bollard, the audience is gently led to that conclusion. Or even misled, for, given a general similarity in shape and colour, the close-ups could be of a different boat. It is much better, of course, if it is the same boat, but an innocent deception can produce a more satisfactory result than absolute truth.

This is the type of explanatory shot that can often be filmed afterwards, to fill in a gap you may find during editing (see Chapter 7). Perhaps not of the fishing harbour – it may be too far away. But supposing that you are short of a close-up or two for your beach sequence, you can get your subjects to put on the same costumes and photograph their heads against the sky almost anywhere – in the garden, at the swimming pool or on another bit of anonymous beach. You have to be careful with your colour, though. Try, too, to have the light conditions as nearly as possible the same.

Link shots

If a film is to have a smooth outline, the different sequences need to be linked by shots that show the connection between them. This would be the purpose of the bow-wave and wake shots in the sea film, whether you are at sea or have filmed a river trip. They can be followed, if you are on the sort of ship that provides printed programmes, by shots of the programmes themselves showing the ports of call as they loom up. In the same way, the occasional shot through a car windscreen or a train window, though very prone to camera shake, can show movement.

Again, in the description of the holiday film, I suggested that in addition to being the centre of interest in some parts, your companions can provide links by strolling casually past whatever is then the main attraction. It shows that they are still there, and that the parts of the film really are connected.

In a study of a small area there may well be some prominent building or feature, like the spire or dome of a cathedral, that can be included briefly from a number of angles and distances.

Titles

Titles add enormously to the effectiveness of a film. It is more elegant to open your film with a general title than to have to say 'This is a film about . . .', and similarly it is better to have something that indicates the end rather than a sudden blank screen. In between, the audience often needs some indication of what is going on and where. Indeed, as many have discovered when running through old films, after a time you can be unsure yourself.

Your scope for titling will depend upon the facilities of your camera. Obviously you can do a great deal more if you can take very close-up shots and, as we shall see in a moment, still more if you can take single frames. Nevertheless, much titling, both displayed and unobtrusive, can be done without a special close-up facility, often while you are making the film itself.

When photographing a very well-known place, you may be able to do without an opening title at all. Big Ben or Trafalgar Square places you as firmly in London as the Eiffel Tower does in Paris. In fact, you can carry this further and use such points as the framework of a film. In London you could, for instance, start from Trafalgar Square and then go down the Mall, off into St James's Park, up to Buckingham Palace, through to the Embankment and the Houses of Parliament, along to Tower Bridge and the Tower itself and then back through the City, past the Mansion House to the Law Courts and back to Trafalgar Square along the Strand. There would be plenty of scope for intimate detail and family shots on the way, and you would barely need a written title at all.

Many towns, counties, fairs and functions tend to advertise themselves. Road signs (Welcome to Little Twitterton) and posters (Daytona 500 1979) keep the audience informed without disturbing the smooth running of the film. They are often big enough to photograph on the simplest cameras. Tourist information offices can usually help by giving you access to, or even personal copies of, posters and notices. They exist to publicise the area, and are consequently approachable. They will certainly supply small leaflets and brochures, generally excellently produced, which you can use for close-up work. So, of course, can travel agencies.

Given close-up facilities – and you can often produce a close-up effect by using a zoom lens at its maximum focal length from a distance of a metre or so – your resources are endless. Travel brochures, maps, book covers and almost anything relevant can be used. So can letter sets – magnetic, felt, stencil or transfer types, and children's toys like alphabet blocks.

Some brochures are better than others. Most will give you some kind of title, but I remember a particularly good one in booklet form, showing a series of pictures of a country I was visiting. To signal each move from one place to another, my film showed a page of the booklet turning to a new, named illustration, followed by a similar shot of the place itself. Of course, you don't actually need a booklet to use the general idea, but in that form it certainly works rather well. A travel book or an illustrated guide might be used in the same way, though there is the question of copyright to be considered if you are thinking about showing to a wider audience than just a few friends.

A good, bold map can be used similarly. It should be on the largest scale possible if you are covering a small area in detail, but a general map is better if you are moving through a large area or a whole country. You really want one with not much more detail than you are actually going to use; a complete street plan of a city or meticulous survey of a larger area is rarely as effective as the sort of semi-sketch map that shows important towns and points of interest, often decorated with little drawings, with some indication of how they are connected. If nothing suitable is available, you could produce a map with the aid of tracing paper and a little skill and patience.

Your map can be used as a general introduction, and then reintroduced from time to time, marked to show your route and the places appearing in the following sequence. The marks need to be strong, clear and as neat as possible: they

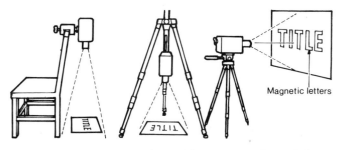

Magnetic letters

Any piece of lettering, printed material or poster can be made into a title, but the camera must be firmly fixed to produce a steady image

are going to be magnified on the screen, and quite small irregularities will show up. To allow correction, and indeed to save destroying your map, the marks can be made in chinagraph pencil on a sheet of glass or clear plastic laid over it, but in this case you will have to take care to avoid reflections when shooting.

Any form of lettering can be used for verbal titles. The size of lettering needed will depend on how close up your camera will focus – the farther away you are the larger the letters will have to be. The simpler and shorter you can make the wording the better; more than three or four lines of writing will be less than ideally legible on projection. If you want each title to be quite individual, you can stencil or transfer them, or even write them yourself if your script is good enough.

Alternatively you can use magnetic or felt letters, and this is often quicker and neater, besides being more economical of materials. Felt letters that stick to a felt background are specially made for titling, but you can get a series called 'Fuzzy Felt' made for children to play with. The same manufacturer supplies sets of coloured shapes for making patterns, and these could be used in combination with letters in appropriate circumstances. Some such arrangement is especially apt for films about children, but you can also build up a cartoon-like sketch of a vaguely relevant scene and use it as a backgound to all your subtitles in the same film. There is no end to the ways in which you can vary your titles with quite simple resources, though of course you don't want them so elaborate as to distract attention from the film itself. After all, that is the opposite of their purpose.

There is one golden rule in making up verbal titles: *avoid a white background*. You will have noticed that captions in old silent films are always in white letters on a black ground. This is because black letters on a white ground simply do not show up properly; the white screen glares at the audience and dazzles them. In simple titles the best way is to follow the old example. You can, of course, make coloured titles, in which case the background should be dark and the lettering light, rather than the other way round.

Cumulative titles
If your camera can take single frames, you can build up your titles letter by letter. First of all set up the camera and background so that both stay absolutely still. Then put one letter – or one word if you like – on the background and expose two or perhaps three frames. Add the next piece and expose the same number of frames and so on until your title is complete, when you run the whole thing for long enough

for its message to be absorbed as a whole – not necessarily very long, but for much longer than the intervals between the pieces. Remember that you will be projecting at 18 frames per second, so with a two-frame interval you will be putting up letters at the rate of nine every second.

In a similar way, you can animate your map titles. Show the map, then ink in a little of the route, take two frames and so on until you reach your immediate destination. This has been called a 'slug map', because you leave a trail in the same way that a slug does.

Photographing your titles
The reason for holding both camera and title card in the same places when making cumulative titles is obvious: if either moves, the title will dance about on the screen while it is being assembled. There is no way of putting your camera back in the same position once it has been altered. Equally, of course, no movement should occur while you are filming an ordinary title. It looks silly if it jumps or judders.

For still, non-cumulative titles you can manage quite well by putting your card on the floor and resting your camera, pointing downwards, on the back of a chair or a rung of a step ladder. This, though, is very definitely second best to using a tripod either for downward shots or, so long as you can make your title stand exactly upright, for horizontal ones. It is most important that your material should be *exactly* parallel to the plane of your film: at such close quarters it will show badly if it is not. Shooting horizontally, it is best to pin your material to a wall or a door, and arrange your shot to exclude the pins. Alternatively, it is possible (though tricky) to stand your material on a music rack or something similar, and give your camera a corresponding tilt.

The light on the subject needs to be very even and without shadows. The floor just inside a french window can be suitable, but better still is the step outside when there is no direct sunlight – and no wind to blow your material away. Needless to say, the card must be exactly centred. There is no problem about this with a reflex viewfinder, but with a separate-window viewfinder physical measurement is the only real answer; at such close range a non-reflex finder cannot be accurate. You can check your position reasonably easily if you use the vertical set-up and hold a weighted string under the exact centre of the lens. If the card is so placed that the string points to its exact centre, all will be well.

There are, not surprisingly, various devices on the market to ease this task. Basically, they all consist of a camera mounting block on a track that leads to an upright easel. The camera is pushed right forward on the track, the easel is adjusted so that the lens is exactly in its centre, and then the camera is moved back to a suitable taking distance. The easel may be equipped only for lettering, or it may accommodate other matter as well. It usually has provision for two shaded lamps, one at each side, to take care of the evenness of lighting. This type of equipment can take much of the fuss out of titling, provided that the track is no shorter than your camera's minimum focusing distance. You normally need to be able to focus down to less than a metre.

7

Editing

Shortly after you have sent your film off for processing, back comes a neat little packet containing exactly what you have taken, with a leader strip in front so that you see all your film, not just most of it. Unless you are a much better photographer than I am, you find, on projecting it, that you have some good shots, some bad ones and some indifferent. You will also probably find that the various scenes do not, or do not all, follow on smoothly. What you have, in fact, is some of the bones of your skeleton.

You will certainly want to cut out the bad bits, for which the only essential tool is a splicer. This is a gadget that cuts your film for you and holds it still while you stick the ends together. There are two sorts. One makes an end-to-end joint with the aid of special strips of sticky tape perforated to match the film. The other has a scraper to remove the emulsion from a narrow strip at one end of the film, and makes a lap joint with the aid of special cement. The former is said to be easier but – perhaps because I am long used to the latter – I do not find it so. I also find that the joins show up more than with the cement method.

Only just less than essential is a viewer. This is normally a hand-operated device that allows you to move the film at any speed you choose while projecting a small image on to a ground-glass screen. It has a punch for marking the frame at which you want to cut, and you can move the film backwards and forwards until you are satisfied that it is at exactly the right frame.

You *can* edit using your projector, but this is more cumbersome, especially with modern types where the film disappears into mysterious plastic labyrinths before emerging at the far end. There is little difficulty in locating where one sequence ends and another begins, but much more difficulty in choosing where to cut an overlong shot. There are also problems in locating the odd frame or couple of frames where a head bobbed up or where there is an inexplicable blur, and this is where the editor-viewer is invaluable. You might think that one rogue frame does not matter, but it is surprising how it shows up.

Constructive editing

If you have accepted the arguments already made in favour of film planning, you will agree that there is much more to editing than just cutting out the bad bits. You have to take your shots when the conditions are right, and more often than not they will be in a less than ideal order for the screen. Take, for instance, the cruise film. This has certain fixed points, like the port visits, that must logically be shown in the order they happened. But shipboard activities and wake shots are not, in themselves, dated. So you can fit them in between the fixed points so as to keep the interest up and maintain variety. It won't matter to your audience – or to you after a time – that a particular game actually took place before and not after Naples, so long as you don't have the finals before the heats.

This is the time too, to get your varied shots of the same scene in the right order. We said that changes of angle add interest to films, but agreed that it is not often possible to make the shots in the ideal order. Editing gives you the opportunity to cut your close-up heads into the beach game sequence, and to extract from it the caught ball and put it at the end. Dramatic moments have to be filmed when they happen, which is rarely the most effective moment for the finished product. You can reshape your sequence, without violence to its essential truth, so that it does form a rounded episode.

The sort of sequence we are talking about is described in Chapter 3 with special references to a harbour scene and to photographing buildings. How you achieve it depends on you, but it may help if you imagine yourself leaning on that harbour wall (unless of course you have a real one handy to practise on) and watching the boat come in. Your eyes will wander about, taking in the whole view. There is your

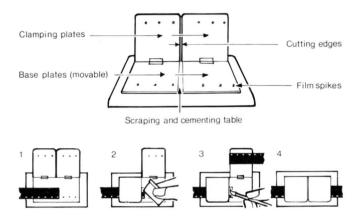

Clamping plates

Cutting edges

Base plates (movable)

Film spikes

Scraping and cementing table

Joining films calls for a splicer. Cement splices are the least obtrusive. The splicer cuts off the film to give a small overlap (1); scrape the emulsion off the lower end with a blade or the built-in scraper (2); apply film cement (3) and drop the other flap down (4)

opening long shot. Then perhaps you look along the quay at a group of fishermen. Amongst them one attracts your interest (middle shot and close up). A look at the waves lapping against the wall, followed by another look to see where the boat has got to, and so on. Eventually a little flurry of activity as she comes alongside – how neatly the mooring lines settle on the bollard – and then the fish are being discharged. Another long view and you wander away.

When photographing, you should have shot most of the component parts of this sequence, but probably not in the most effective order. This is partly because the camera cannot concentrate its attention as your eye can. If you think about it you will realise that by concentrating you actually do see long shots, middle shots and close-ups with the naked eye. Further, while photographing you will have moved about to get different views of parts of the scene. Now, while cutting, is your opportunity to shape the sequence as though you could have been in several places at once, and build it into a harmonious whole.

Pace
In cutting you can also control the pace and rhythm of your film, building up excitement or producing serenity. Broadly, the longer your shots – this side of boredom – the more peaceful the effect, while quick cutting makes for excitement. When the goody and the baddy are dashing to save or slaughter the girl, the film cross-cuts quickly to show their progress; when the goody bails her out there is a long, slow reunion scene.

Your harbour scene can be cut on the same principles. It can open with fairly leisurely looks at everything around, move into shorter and shorter shots as the boat comes alongside, relaxing to longer shots as the excitement dies down. Similar considerations apply to all your sequences and all your films.

This style of cutting, for pace and action, becomes even more important when we edit narrative and story films. You can improve a holiday record tremendously by good cutting; bad cutting can completely ruin a story. An overlong shot at a crucial moment loses the audience's attention, but one not long enough fails to make its point. We shall take this point more fully in the chapter on narrative films, but it is worth noting for all purposes now. You are out to make a film that interests its audience: don't let them get bored, but equally let each scene make its effect. It is a matter of judgement and experience.

The practical side

The first stage is to go back to your original spools and run through them. Make notes of the scenes they show and their order. You can then shuffle them on paper, as it were, and relist them in the order you think best. Do not bother about comparative length at first, just the order.

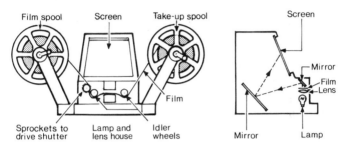

A viewer allows easy selection of the right places to cut

Now you can start with your viewer and splicer, cutting at the appropriate places. Now is the time, too, to pick out the odd bad frames and get rid of them. For this latter purpose you cut and splice immediately, but the question of order cannot be dealt with quite so quickly. You can't stick the bits together until you have cut them up. So as you cut each piece you mark it and store it temporarily. Some people do this with the aid of a numbered row of panel pins. You hang piece two by the end perforation on pin two, and so on for the rest until you are ready to start gluing. Very effective, but it does need an undisturbed working area. I prefer to roll each bit up either on an old spool or in a bit of paper, with the name and number of the shot on the outside. The exact method doesn't matter in the least, so long as you know what you are doing. You must avoid having unidentified strips of film all over the room if you want to avoid a headache.

Having sorted the lot out, you simply get a large reel and wind the pieces on as you stick them together. Put a piece of

107

white leader strip at the end as well as at the beginning: it protects the film and prevents a sudden glare on the screen when you get to the end.

As a matter of practice, I prefer to start this process with only one or two reels. Then, having dealt with them, I can edit the next into the first two and so on. It means that you have to cut and recut, but this is not of great consequence, because you only lose one frame – one-eighteenth of a second – each time. It avoids having a vast number of bits of film lying about waiting, and I find that I can see the structure building up as I work. Sometimes this gives me better ideas about the general treatment.

The next step
So far we have done nothing about the length of shots. In fact we have got as far as what the professionals call a 'rough cut'. Quite right too: you can't do everything at once. The film should have taken shape, but not necessarily its final shape. So run the film though once again, with your most critical eye. Try to imagine what it will look like in ten years' time. In addition to possible improvements in the order, you are now looking for pieces that don't quite fit, pieces that go on too long, and pieces that do not explain themselves adequately.

In making a rough cut you will have removed any really bad patches and thrown them away, and you will have put on one side shots that clearly belong to a different film – either because you have been shooting for more than one film on the same reel, or because an irresistible opportunity cropped up. Now you are looking for shots that seemed relevant at the time, but now disturb the flow. Remove these too and put them on one side: you can always put them back again if you change your mind, or use them in a different film.

Of course you try to make your shots about the right length when you take them, but you don't always succeed, and in any case it is better to start with them too long than too short. You can always cut, but you can't lengthen. Now is the time to decide how much of any shot is enough. It is a matter of judgement, and this faculty is one of the things that decides whether you are in the Eisenstein or the pot-boiler class of film makers. The most stringent mentors will tell you to cut every frame and every shot that does not add something positive to the film – when in doubt, cut it out. But you may well feel that you are not in competition with Eisenstein, and decide to allow yourself the luxury of keeping a pleasant shot, or letting it run a little, whether or not it could be cut by the strictest criteria. On the other hand, too much self-indulgence will spoil your film. Again, as with possible irrelevancies, a cut is not irrevocable; you can put the piece back if on second thoughts you prefer to have it in.

A film should explain itself without the need for a running commentary. You may find, as you run through, that at times that does not happen. Make notes of the times and places, because you can often fill the gaps with a little extra photography, as already discussed in Chapter 6.

For the moment, make your additional changes. There is no need to be shy about cutting and re-cutting. Properly-made splices last for years, and cine film is tough enough to stand a great deal of reasonably careful handling. Go on working until you are satisfied with the results.

Salvage

Having taken a look at the methods of constructing a film from the beginning, we might now think about the bags of bones in the cupboard. These are all those spools full of interesting photographs and reminiscences that somehow seem unsatisfactory on the screen, and frequently remain in the cupboard unprojected for that very reason. This is a pity, because there is bound to be good material there, and after all a poor spool costs just as much to produce as a good one.

The odds and ends are unsatisfactory, in all probability, because of trigger-happiness. This is a disease from which few amateur cinephotographers are ever totally immune, but it is commonest, naturally, when the camera is a new toy. Seeing a fascinating scene, you shoot it without considering how it will fit in with other shots, with what can come before and after it. Sometimes, taken by surprise, you loose off without thinking about the light, or composition, or even whether your stance is firm enough to hold the camera completely still. The result is spools of film containing varied shots, mostly interesting in themselves but some imperfect, that are not related in any logical way and therefore make little impact when shown.

The crucial fault, in fact, is to forget the difference between still and cine work. Still cameras produce photographs that are looked at in isolation, as entities in themselves, while cine films are shown in sequence on the screen; unless there is some reasonable connection between one sequence and the next they lose their full effect.

The counsel of perfection, of course, is never to take a shot unless you know beforehand that it will be of some use. Few of us are perfect, though, and besides it often seems a pity to miss an unrepeatable shot simply because you cannot immediately think of a home for it. Fortunately, there is at least a palliative: you can go through the miscellanea and, with the help of a few titles and perhaps some additional new shots, construct a film backwards as it were. It probably won't be as good as a fully planned film, but with luck, time and patience it will be reasonably effective, and the job itself is interesting and rewarding.

Starting the reconstruction

If you are going to try to wrest order out of chaos, first have a close look at the chaos and analyse it. In other words, run the films through. Sometimes it helps to splice them all together on to one big reel in date order; at other times you can manage equally well without.

It pays to see the films at least three times before getting down to any sorting. The first time, remind yourself of what is there; the second time, try to assess the scenes and their subjects; the third time, make notes on paper, or (perhaps better) speak them into a tape recorder, if you have one handy. Then you are not trying to look at both the screen and the paper at the same time, and you can transcribe later. You should end up with a list that might run something like this:

1 Children in garden	Fair
2 Mary washing up	Darkish
3 Children going out on bikes	Good
4 Baker delivering bread	Fair, but a bit fuzzy
5 Children coming back	Good
6 Swings in park	Goodish
7 Park lake – pan	Good, but wobbles
8 High street	Fair
9 Mary hanging out washing	Good
10 Dog barking	Fair
11 Dog wagging tail	Good
12 ? Park again	Blurred
13 Park lake – children with boats	Good
14 Picnic tea in garden	Good

and so on.

Naturally, while running the films through you will have been thinking about what to do with them. Now, examining the list, you can crystallise your ideas a little. Two or three shots it would be best to discard altogether, like the blurred one of the park. The rest might well go into two groups – round the house and at the park – though they could, at a pinch, be fused into one. In either case they will need supplementing a bit, but that's quite possible so long as the children have not grown up too much in the interval.

Now there is really only a minor degree of chaos in the list. In fact any really good collection of old bones will contain a much more heterogeneous collection of shots, and will probably need sorting under three or four headings, including 'don't know what to do with it'. Let us divide this lot into two, to show the general method. We can start by making three more lists, under the heads of House, Park, and Horrible, at the same time trying to put the shots into a sensible order. They might be like these:

House

9	Mary hanging out washing	A1
10	Dog barking	A2
4	Baker delivering	A3
11	Dog wagging tail	A4
8	High street	A5
1	Children in garden	A6
14	Picnic tea	A7
2	Mary washing up	A8

Park

3	Children going out	B1
6	Swings in park	B2
13	Park lake, children	B3
5	Children coming back	B4

Horrible

7	Park lake pan
12	Blurred bit

Neither of these sequences is really complete, but assemble them for the moment, even though some of the shots are a bit doubtful, and see them again before deciding on the next move. Notice that each shot has been given a new number within its new sequence. Jot those numbers down on the original list, then chop the films up and label the pieces with the new numbers. This is where you are very liable to land up with a room full of film strips at bedtime if you are not careful, so it is very important to do something with each piece as you cut it. The pinboard system works well provided that you have enough pins, but only if the board can stay undisturbed if you are interrupted or get tired. You may prefer the roll and label method: the little packages can easily be put in a box or a drawer until next time.

The next step, obviously, is to stick the pieces together in the right order. Since they are all labelled, this should be no problem, and if you are very well organised it is convenient to splice from the end of the sequence to the beginning, rather than the other way on. Then your completed film is ready to show, whereas if you do it the other way round you will have to rewind it first.

During the sorting process you will probably find that you have some spare strips of white leader film. Remember that if you put one at the end as well as at the beginning, you will not only save your film from damage, but also ensure that you do not have a sudden white glare from the screen at the end of the film.

Rounding off
Having spliced the pieces together, run the results through again. This time you are looking for possible improvements. These could be additional shots, better versions of existing shots, changes in shot lengths, and possibly titles.

Additional shots would belong to the same category as those mentioned in Chapter 6. In the case of the 'House' film you could add point to the High Street scene – otherwise rather an intrusion – by surrounding it by shots of Mary leaving the house, shopping in the High Street, and return-ing. Then later on she could be shown preparing the picnic tea and bringing it out. During the tea you could add, if you had not already got them, one or two close-up shots of children reaching for sandwiches and eating them. The park film obviously needs to be longer: perhaps you could have another go at the lake shot that was discarded as too shaky, and add a few more attractions, whatever they may be, with the children featuring whenever suitable.

As for better versions of existing shots, the original list notes that the baker was a bit fuzzy, and Mary washing up rather dark. Reshoot until you are satisfied, or anyway think you have done enough. There is one thing to remember in supplementary shooting: all conditions (weather, background, trinkets and especially clothes) should be as nearly the same as in the original shots as possible – unless, of course, there is an obvious reason for the difference.

The need, or at any rate the usefulness, of titles has already been stressed, as has the nice question of shot lengths. You are trying to make an interesting film of your own reminiscences mainly for your own amusement, so opinions can vary, but if the aim of interest is to be achieved, very lengthy shots may need cutting. It always seems a shame to throw away good film, but few people really want to watch a ship's wake for minutes on end. However pleasant live, it is a long time on the screen.

Rag-bags

You may find that after sorting a number of spools you still have shots that do not fit anywhere. Only the most self-disciplined photographer never takes an irrelevant shot. You can always put remainders in a rag-bag film. It will not be a real film, just an animated scrap album, but you might like to see it now and again, and some of the shots may even come in useful for films to come.

8

Narrative films

Every film should tell a story, but where the story is the point of the film, rather than the link between photographs of interesting people and places, even more care is needed over planning and continuity, and much cooperation and a modicum of acting ability are required from the cast.

The starting point, as always, is a clear plot that explains itself in pictures. Sound or captions can help, but we are making pictures, not plays, and the audience's attention will always be principally upon what they can see. As a simple and obvious example, a character might jump up and say 'Look – the baddies'. If we were depending on words, the next shot might be the same character bound and gagged. But the real next shot is, of course, the baddies, previously identified by black masks or whatever. You can enhance the atmosphere of your film by using words and music, but the pictures and not the sound should always be the main element.

We shall be considering the use of sound in more detail later, but one point is worth making here. Automatic-recording-level systems (those that are controlled solely by the camera without the need for a second person supervising the recording) are effective only when the sound you want to record is predominant. They will record a band, for instance, but will manage dialogue only when it is very close to the microphone and there are not too many other noises, and even then there are problems. There are ways round them, and the apparatus can be most useful, but it is unlikely on its own to produce satisfying soundtracks for complete films.

Preliminary thoughts

As a preparation for sketching out a completely fictional film, let us think about a halfway stage – a day in the life of, say, a small girl. Granted that the story is subordinate here, you still have to have a degree of consistency if the result is to look like only one day, and you still have to have cooperation from the star for many of the shots.

A careful structure – packing all the action into one day – can give ordinary family films an intriguing narrative feel

The framework might be getting up and dressing, breakfast, meeting friends, going to nursery school, playing with toys, dolls or a pet, a walk with mother, tea in the garden and going to bed. Now, at least for the getting-up and going-to-bed shots, you need cooperation and (preferably) an attempt at acting from the infant. You can't do them if she is camera-shy, but if she is happy to join in you can have a lot of fun and also gain a bit of experience in directing actors. My own daughter, at two, revelled in the idea and, lighting being a problem, cheerfully went to 'sleep' with a broad grin on her face in the middle of the afternoon. The shot is clearly a fake, but it rounds the film off well.

For continuity's sake, your star should come home from school dressed in the clothes she went in, and should come

out in the same sort of weather as you had in the morning –
unless you show a gathering storm in between. You will find,
too, that you need something between the beginning and the
end of school to indicate the passing of time. It could,
perhaps, be a shot through the classroom window, or
preparations for a meal at home, and possibly a clock face.
Without something like this it may appear that she has just
dropped in to collect a bag of sweets.

This sort of film, naturally, depends entirely on what the
subject really does do, perhaps not every day but reasonably
often. It also gives opportunities to include pictures of your
house, your garden, and your surroundings. Moreover, it
gives you useful experience in moulding circumstances to fit
a story line, albeit sketchy, instead of allowing the line to be
dictated by circumstances.

What sort of story?

Moving from semi-reportage to full-scale fiction involves a
great deal of preparation. First of all you have to decide on
your story. If you are inventive, you might wish to make up
something that suits the people and materials you have
available. A treasure-hunt theme, for instance, could allow
you to include a number of local places of interest, as could a
'little boy lost and found' theme. Equally, you could select an
episode from some well-loved book and work it into a script.
But whatever you choose you must be able to show in
pictures. Moreover, it must be comparatively short, or you
will exhaust everybody's patience.

Plays seem obvious sources, but they are deceptive ones
since they depend on words. So anything that you select you
must first translate into pictorial terms. After all, some
commercial films depend almost entirely on what you see;
any sound is incidental. You may remember *The Red Balloon*
– a simple story of a child whose magic balloon followed him
through the streets until it was finally punctured by other
envious children who chased the owner to a scrap heap,

116

where he was rescued by a cloud of balloons and flown away high into the sky. Not a word was spoken. You have also surely seen *Tom and Jerry* cartoon films, where the sound complements but does not do much to explain the action. Again, though one hesitates to pray in aid such a classic mime, Charlie Chaplin tells long and complicated stories with no, or very few, words. Of course, with a sophisticated sound system, you can add a lot to a film, but even then the pictures must come first.

Very well, first catch your story – but let it not be too long, too wordy, too complicated or, unless you have special resources, dependent upon costume. *Vanity Fair* and *Twelfth Night* are out. Something from a comic strip is nearer the mark.

The following tale is from the *Decameron* (Fifth Day, Third Tale). Boccaccio's themes have been adapted by Chaucer, Shakespeare, Keats, Tennyson and hundreds of others. He is by no means always indecorous, and even where he is the plot may often be adaptable for a respectable family film – his characters' stratagems can be turned to other purposes. He has the great virtue of being succinct and to the point; moreover he is in no position to argue about what you do to his work. This particular tale is perfectly proper in the original. Noble Roman and (wealthy) plebeian girl. Neither family will agree to their marriage so they elope on horseback. They are attacked by a band of robbers who capture the boy; the girl gallops off but gets lost. She finds shelter in a humble cottage and, after a further narrow escape from robbers, is taken to a friend of both families. Meanwhile another band of robbers has attacked the first, and the boy gets away in the confusion. He tries to follow the girl, but gets lost and spends the night up a tree. In the morning he is guided by shepherds to – fortunately – the same house where the girl now is. Friend pacifies both families, and they marry and live happily ever afterwards.

This is no good as it stands unless you have considerable resources and more patience. But it can be put into modern dress, and adapted to whatever resources you have at hand. Let us try.

Planning the story

Boy meets girl – at school, club or anywhere. Boy's strict church-going parents object to girl's freethinking family (but the parental quarrel is not essential). The two meet and go off for a day in the country, but have wayside accident. Girl goes off to get help, but takes the wrong turning (signpost obscured by lorry?). Girl rescued by passing motorist (could be at roadside café) and taken to next village. As they arrive at

When making a fiction film, see each scene as a stage in telling the story

the post office, boy descends from bus, very worried because he has not seen girl on the road. Happy reunion; telephone home; all's well. The wayside accident would depend on the means of transport, but let us suggest bicycles, and a lost chain-link (easy to repair, but no-one ever carries a spare).

The essential cast list for this epic would be a boy, a girl and a passing motorist, with parents as optional extras. The essential sites are home, a country road with a fork, and a post office with a bus stop – preferably far enough from home to make the adventure credible to people with local knowledge. Provided that all these are available, you can go on to draft a shooting script. This involves breaking the story down into sequences, and planning a series of shots in each sequence. It might start something like this:

Boy and girl leave club or school

(a) Long shot	Exterior of building.	
(b) Mid-shot	Doors (opening if possible) and youngsters coming out, narrowing to:	
(c) Near shot	Boy and girl together.	
(d) Close up	Faces of two in animated conversation, or absorbed in each other.	
(d) Mid-shot	Backs of two, with parents approaching. They receive pair coldly, and one walks off dejectedly.	
(e) Close-up	The other's disappointed face.	
(f) Mid-shot	Arrival home: door closes, lights seen to go on through window.	

Pause for thought here. Facial expressions call for acting ability. If the shot doesn't quite come off, consider a stamp of the foot, and child leaving ahead of parents, who glance at each other and hurry after. If a large enough cast is available, both sets of parents could arrive and mime disapproval of each other – turning away sharply, perhaps. If the window shot is taken late in the day, fade out by using the diaphragm.

The appointment

(a) Another day	General shot of, say, milkman in street, to make the point.
(b) Mid-shot	Front door: child comes out.
(d) Long shot	Two seen parting, a bit furtively, outside the club building.
(c) Close-up	Girl's hand holding a note, which she opens and reads. (You can show the text of the note – 'meet me at Hogg's Corner' – if you like, but it isn't essential.)

The meeting

(a) Long shot	Hogg's Corner (if you are identifying the place in the note, choose a name that can

	be illustrated: Mr Hogg's shop at Hogg's Corner, say; or you could name a pub, then show the pub sign). Boy with bicycle.
(b) Mid-shot	Boy fiddling with bicycle as girl approaches. He looks up.
(c) Close-up	Defective or badly fitted chain link.
(d) Mid-shot	Boy points up the road, and they ride off.

You carry on in this way through the remaining sequences, which are clearly the chain falling off, the girl riding off and taking the wrong road, the boy pushing his bicycle, the girl being taken back to the right road and the meeting outside the post office. You add, at intervals, if you wish, scenes of worried parents eventually getting together, cross-cutting between one scene and another. Finally, there will be a shot of the two in a telephone box, perhaps, or reunion at home.

This type of skeleton story leaves you quite free to elaborate in your own way on some basic and simple theme. The other way is to take a fully written story and adapt it to your needs. Here you will have to rewrite the text almost completely, expressing thoughts and conversations in visual terms. This is not always easy, which is why professional films from books so often do not satisfy lovers of the books themselves. But you, of course, are seeking to satisfy yourself and your immediate circle rather than a wide circle of critics, and if you wish to film a piece of *Swallows and Amazons* you will have enormous fun trying.

No-one should have any doubt that making a story film demands considerable application and work, pleasurable though it is. You will not get all your shots on one day. You will also have more than the usual editing to do. All this needs a much more than casual interest in the hobby, and assistance would be valuable. You can get help quite easily by joining a local cine club, where members are always glad to advise and instruct, and perhaps to recruit you as an assistant on a story-film team. This will give you experience as well as enjoyment.

9

Sound

Nowadays, we all see films and television programmes with appropriate sound linked to the pictures. The words come exactly as the actors speak, and the effects just at the right moments. Sound is so much a part of visual entertainment that we can hardly imagine its absence, so we miss it if our own films are shown in silence. After all, when silent films were shown in cinemas they were usually accompanied by more or less appropriate music from piano or orchestra, and the same can be true of our own.

You can make a very effective soundtrack with music and commentary, without trying to reproduce the actual sound occurring at any moment, but it still needs to be synchronised with the film itself. It is tempting to think that you can do this on a separate tape recorder, and play film and tape together, but unfortunately it doesn't work: however careful your preparation, one or the other gets ahead. You can always stop one to let the other catch up, but it isn't exactly a smooth performance. You must have some sort of coupling between tape and projector to make such a system effective. To provide for this need, the manufacturers have produced sound systems for amateur films. They can be incredibly effective, but their use calls for much more attention to detail than is needed for silent cine-photography.

Super 8 sound cameras record on a magnetic stripe down the side of the film, which is the equivalent of the tape in a tape recorder. There are also devices on the market that enable you to couple a tape recorder to a silent camera.

Either will record any sound – I repeat, *any* sound – that occurs during photography and, in conjunction with the appropriate apparatus, will reproduce it in exact time with the photographs that it accompanies. In perfect circumstances, either system will produce perfect results. Alas, perfection is beyond the reach of most of us; we will discuss later how nearly we can attain it.

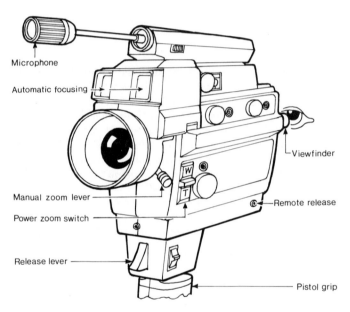

Sound and picture are recorded simultaneously in a single-system camera.

The complement to the sound camera is, of course, the sound projector. The standard sound projector reproduces the sound on the film stripe. This is the best type to use because of its utter simplicity. There are other projector systems, but they depend on ancillary equipment; so, of course, do other camera systems, but while it is one thing to fiddle about with extra apparatus while you are filming, it is quite another to fiddle about while you are screening your films. So, for reproduction purposes, simplest is best – even though it may be possible to reach better acoustical standards by more complicated processes. You may prefer to use, as many people (including myself) do, systems other than stripe to make your recordings, since there is little difficulty in transferring the sound on to stripe on the final film.

Now, two types of sound are heard in films: one is the sound of people talking and singing, and the other is background music and commentary – a sophisticated version of the piano in silent cinema. Most large-scale films contain a mixture of both, but many excellent shorter films (especially those concerned with nature) rely entirely on soundtracks made later to fit the film, rather than on the actual sounds heard when shooting. Both types of track work well, but both depend on accurate, or at least fairly accurate, synchronisation between film and sound.

Analysing all this, we realise that in producing soundtracks for films, there are three processes involved: recording the sound (whether live or recorded later), tying it in with the film, and reproducing it exactly when it should be heard. Each of these processes needs care and attention. Let us look first at the apparatus available, then at the construction of soundtracks, and finally at what is probably the trickiest of the lot, the recording of live sound at the same time as you are taking photographs.

Sound cameras

Super 8 sound film is like silent Super 8 film but with a band (stripe) of magnetic oxide running along each edge. The wider stripe is intended for recording a soundtrack. The narrow stripe is there to even out the thickness of the film so that it winds true on to its spool. Although the production specifications of the second (balance) stripe are variable, it is now commonly used to provide a second recording track for the final film.

123

Sound cameras record on the wider stripe. They accept prestriped (sound) film in special cartridges, which are larger than normal Super 8 cartridges. Sound cartridges have a second aperture that allows the camera sound head (which is like a tape-recorder head) to contact the stripe. When the camera is running, the sound is recorded at a point on the stripe 18 frames ahead of the picture. While silent cameras cannot accommodate sound cartridges, sound cameras all accept silent cartridges.

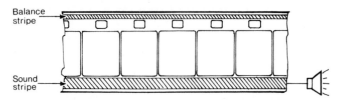

Magnetic coatings allow sound to be recorded on Super 8 film; they can be applied during manufacture or added later. The balance stripe allows the film to lie flat on its reel, and is also magnetic

The main attraction of a sound camera is that you can record events in your life – children playing, special occasions and so on – with live sound. Just hook up the microphone and shoot away. You capture all the sounds as you film, each one exactly synchronised with the picture, ready to play back as soon as the film is processed.

On the face of it, this is the ultimate in simple convenience. You have a single piece of equipment to carry, and the sound is automatically synchronised with the picture: it has to be, since it is recorded on the film.

Unfortunately, stripe sound introduces editing problems, as we see later. Even more unfortunately, the microphone cannot distinguish between baby's chatter, which you want, and next door's dog barking, which you don't. So the recording of live sound demands more care and attention than one might think; that is true for *any* system of live sound recording.

124

Sound projectors

Naturally, sound projectors work very like sound cameras:
the sound head is positioned 18 frames ahead of the picture
gate. Thus if you put a reel of sound film straight from the
processors on to a sound projector, the soundtrack plays
with the picture.

Sound projectors can record as well as play back, so you
can add sound to your films whenever the camera sound is
unsatisfactory. In fact, there is no need to record on all – or
even any – of a sound film when shooting. You can simply
add the unsynchronised soundtrack later, when you have
edited your material to produce the film you want.

To complicate matters, sound projectors come in three
degrees of sophistication. The simplest have a single record/
replay head that works on the main stripe. They often have
mixing and superimposing controls, but they all pose one
danger. It is only too easy to erase your live sound while you
are adding extra material. When it is good, your camera-
recorded sound is priceless. Once wiped out, or recorded
over, it is gone forever. So it is far better to leave it alone
altogether. However, if you must add material using this type
of projector, first copy your live sound on to a separate tape.
If disaster befalls, you won't be able to put it back exactly in
synchronisation (unless you use synchronised tape) but at
least you have something.

A much more secure way is to use a projector with
twin-track sound heads. This allows you to choose between
the normal stripe and the balance stripe for your recording.
When you are adding material to existing live sound, record
the new material on the balance stripe. That way your original
material is quite safe.

The most sophisticated projectors have separate amplifiers
for each track. This allows you, again, to add material without
disturbing your in-camera sound. It also allows you to
produce stereophonic sound if you want it.

A sound projector is well worth considering even if you
have a silent camera. Any film, old or new, can have a stripe
added to it, and this can be used for dubbing any sort of

sound you want on to the film. Also, you can buy or hire commercially-made sound films for special occasions. The range available should allow you to cater for any sort of gathering from a toddler's Christmas party to a full-scale orgy.

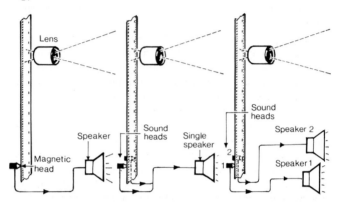

The original aim of magnetic-stripe Super 8 was to provide a single recording track. With a two-head projector, material can also be recorded on the balance stripe and mixed with the main stripe sound during projection. With two amplifiers, twin-head 'stereo' projectors can provide two separate sound channels

Even if you use one of the more complicated mechanical or electronic tape–film coupling systems (see later), you should aim to end up with your soundtrack recorded on the film. It is so much more convenient, and more reliable. The other major advantage is that all 'stripe' projectors use the same system; you can project any Super 8 sound film on any Super 8 sound projector. Of course, the simpler models will not replay sound on the balance stripe; so with those you hear only part of the soundtrack when each stripe has different material.

Recording controls

The exact degree of control you have when recording depends on the controls on your camera or projector. The simplest cameras have an automatic level (or 'gain') control (ALC or AGC) to give you an optimum recording level – for reproduction quality, not for aesthetic effect. Some allow you to choose between two or more levels, others give you full control.

Projectors, too, have ALC, and most offer a recording gain control as an alternative so that you can select the recording level to suit the material. Most, too, have a superimpose (sound-on-sound) control, with which you can add to an existing soundtrack. The variations, though, are considerable. Study very carefully the literature and instructions relating to your equipment before starting. Only when there is no alternative, and you know exactly what you are doing, should you consider recording near your precious live sound.

Sound film stock

Since Super 8 prestriped film in its special cartridges cannot be used in silent cameras, there is some advantage in possessing a sound camera even if you never record with it. It enables you to choose any prestriped material so that you can record your sound track directly on the final edited film. If this is the way you want to work, choose a camera for its picture facilities and ignore the quality of its sound system.

On the other hand, you can work almost equally well with a silent camera, which gives you two ways to achieve stripe sound. You can choose prestriped film in silent cartridges; this is not widely offered, but you can get it if you insist. Alternatively you can have your film striped before or after editing. A reliable photographic dealer can arrange this for you; also several laboratories offer a mail-order service. Film striping is a service that is well worth investigating carefully. Few firms produce a stripe that approaches the quality of prestriped film, so do not just choose the cheapest: find out which is the best.

For the dedicated handyman there are home striping machines. Some fix on preformed stripe (narrow sections of thin recording tape supplied on a reel). One or two spread a band of paste on to the film. Both types require extreme patience to achieve any success at all. Used with extreme care, the preformed type should be more successful than the paste variety. Home striping of films, though, is not a task to be considered lightly; careless handling will certainly produce a poor stripe, and probably make the film unstripeable, if not ruin the pictures as well.

Tape—film coupling systems

Before the advent of sound cameras, enthusiasts used a number of systems for coupling film to tape to provide soundtracks in time (if not in strict synchronisation) with the film. One of the earliest devices available for use with Standard 8 and Super 8 apparatus was designed solely for synchronising sound and film, so that background music and commentary could be added and played back without problems. The tape passed round a bobbin on the projector, and fair synchronisation was maintained by controlling the projector speed to keep the film in step with the tape. It was not always an exact mechanism, but within its limits produced reasonably satisfactory results.

A more elaborate, and very much extant, version of this system uses special tape that has perforations along one side. With their aid, sound can be matched frame by frame. With care and diligence, it is even possible to match live sound – recorded separately but at the time of shooting – to your pictures.

Electric pulse coupling
A more sophisticated system arranges for pulses to be recorded, at the time of shooting, on one track of the tape, one for each frame exposed (or sometimes each two or four frames), through an electrical connection between camera and recorder. At the same time, live sound may be recorded on other tracks; with a suitably equipped projector, this sound will be reproduced in exact synchronisation with the film. Equally, the pulses may be recorded with an empty

camera, and the prepared tape used to record suitable music and commentary, again in exact synchronisation. Clearly, a combination of the two methods is possible on a tape for one film. It is quite simple with the right equipment to transfer the pulse track and the sound from one tape to another. Thus you can edit electronically until you have exactly the right soundtrack. Alternatively, you can edit the tape physically; then add whatever stop/start marks are needed, record the whole on to a tape of suitable format, and use that to reproduce the sound and control the projector speed.

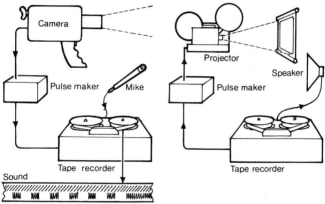

Pulses marking each frame ——long pulse at shot change

Recording sound and timing pulses on a separate tape (open-reel or cassette) provides an alternative but less convenient method of synchronising sound with vision. At one time, 'sound' cameras and projectors incorporated a pulse-sound mechanism

As with the mechanical devices referred to above, the apparatus for this system can be purchased separately from the camera, which itself may need a minor adaptation. Complete systems have been available commercially that provided for pulse signals to be passed between either camera or projector and tape recorder, thus simplifying synchronisation, but they are now discontinued.

The great advantage of the pulse method is that you can edit your picture and sound separately. For reproduction purposes, on the other hand, you are limited to projectors that use the system you have chosen – and there are a number of different systems.

The use of both mechanically and electrically coupled tapes with camera or projector can be referred to, for convenience, as 'double system' sound.

Adding a soundtrack

Ignoring, for the moment, the fascinating complications of live-sound recording and editing, let us consider how to add sound to an existing silent film. In fact, this is really the best way to learn the art of making sound films.

The first need is an accurate time schedule of the film. To get this the projector must be set up exactly in accordance with the manufacturer's instructions for a performance.

If you are using a double system, load the tape, connect up the recorder and select 'playback'. In the case of the pulse system the control pulses should have been already recorded, so that the performance conditions, as far as timing is concerned, are reproduced exactly.

Next, run your film through, noting the matter of each sequence and the time it takes. For this purpose, and indeed for the preparation of the final sound accompaniment, a second tape recorder is extremely useful. While running through you make a click (perhaps with a pencil on the table or on the microphone case itself) at the beginning of each scene, and then describe the scene briefly. After the run-through you time the tape and note the descriptions. Of course you can watch the clock and make pencil notes instead, but I find that the other way is better, because you do not have to watch a screen, a clock, and a piece of paper all at the same time.

The resulting notes will give you a time scale and a series of headings. From this it is possible to decide what, if any, explanatory comments are needed, and the sort of back-

130

ground music that suits each part of the film. All this should be listed, and in particular any commentary should be written down. This helps you to make your remarks concise and clear: if you try to do it from memory you may tend to bumble, repeat yourself and say 'er'. Most of us do in conversation, but coming out of a loudspeaker, especially for the fourth or fifth time, it is tiresome.

The choice of music and other background sound is a matter of individual taste and individual resources. However, you do not want music so strong and powerful that it distracts attention from the film, or, unless the association is particularly apt, so well known that the audience murmur 'I do like – or hate – this tune' instead of watching what is going on. You could happily use a bit of *Tales from the Vienna Woods* for a woodland scene, but if you used *The Blue Danube* for a beach cricket match people would wonder why (although Stanley Kubrick did use it with considerable success in *2001 – A Space Odyssey*).

Copyright

A word of caution should be added here. The obvious sources for your music are gramophone records and tapes, but making copies of them is illegal. In practice, there is no trouble about this if you copy records that you yourself own, and the film is purely for your family and friends. But the moment that you show to a wider audience (which includes schools, clubs, parent-teacher groups, church socials and the like), whether or not any money changes hands, the questions of copyright and performing rights arise. In that case you should take advice or, if you are lucky enough to know some competent amateur musicians, enlist them to play from long-dead composers. But the musicians have to be good: the tape recorder is quite merciless to blunders in performance that are scarcely noticeable live. In addition, there are records on the market that are not subject to reproduction restrictions.

Music and commentary

The lengths to which you go to match music to scene depend partly upon the amount of trouble you are prepared to take, and partly upon the events of the film itself. For instance, in a film about Seville I used a great deal of Albeniz's *Iberia*, but worked in Falla's *Magic Fire* music and *Dance of Terror* for the bullfight scenes and switched to flamenco for the Feria. On the other hand, in a film mainly about quiet country life I used almost the whole of a fairly obscure clarinet quintet by Max Reger.

Let us suppose that you need some variety, and start sketching out a programme for a holiday film. It would go something like this:

Time	Subject	Commentary	Music
0	Car arrives at bungalow: cases out: party leave: cut to beach and bathing.	The sun was shining as we arrived at ... We went straight to the sea.	Mendelssohn: *The Hebrides*
5.15	Beach games: party sunbathes.		Rimsky-Korsakov: Hymn to the Sun from *Coq D'Or*
6.30	Towel down: leave beach: cut to		
7.10	café ...	This was our favourite café, with the crowds passing and the views	Walton: *Portsmouth Point*
	harbour ...	over the harbour and across the square to	Mussorgsky: *The Great*
9.35	cathedral.	the cathedral.	*Gate at Kiev*

For the sake of clarity, I have used fairly well known musical examples here, from the standard classical repertoire, but you will make your own selection according to your tastes. The music does not necessarily change for each comment, and may well change at other points, as at the sunbathing and cathedral shots above.

You can, if you choose, now record this directly on to your final stripe. You will need help, because it is all but impossible to control the records, the recording level and the microphone all at once while watching the timing. If you get the timing wrong, the announcements and changes will be out of step with the events.

Of course the automatic level control is a help, if yours really gives you the recording level that you want, and matches your camera's ALC if you have some live sound. In that case – provided you can work in a room totally insulated from outside noises – you can replay the music through loudspeakers and record it through a microphone. When you speak your commentary over the top, the automatic control will reduce the music volume to ensure that your voice is heard. This is perhaps the simplest way to work as it involves no special connections, but it is also the least flexible.

Virtually all projectors have a 'superimpose' control. So the most logical way to work is to record the music (preferably by direct link, but through speakers and microphone if necessary), then use the superimpose facility to add the commentary directly on the stripe. Once again, if you are recording on the same stripe as your live sound, be quite sure to safeguard that precious material.

Even so, if you have the apparatus available, it is sometimes easier to record the music and commentary first on an intermediate tape constructed to your time schedule. A useful machine for this purpose is the type that permits transfer from one track to another, but other machines have a 'superimpose' button that allows you to introduce new material over the top of earlier.

It is also possible, on a stereo cassette recorder, to feed the music on to one track while speaking on to the other. The two tracks play back together on a monophonic machine, and with the pulse-control system this can be your final tape, the pulses being already recorded on the bottom half. A further transfer will, of course, be needed for stripe.

This, however, is not a recording textbook, and how you actually get the sound on to the final track must depend on your own ingenuity and the apparatus you have available. It is true that the more transfers you make, the lower will be the quality of your final sound. But unless you are using much more elaborate equipment than usual, your sound is not, in any case, going to qualify for a high-fidelity prize, and you should find the deterioration little enough to be acceptable for soundtrack purposes.

Live sound recording

Just as there is more to getting the right picture than aiming in roughly the right direction, there is more to sound recording – and to the effective use of sound with film – than pressing the 'record' button on your machine. If there were not, film companies would not need their elaborate apparatus of sound stages and dubbing studios.

Professional producers do not record their sound on the film at the time of shooting. They make several sound recordings, partly while shooting and partly later, and marry them all with the film in the dubbing studios. Some highly dedicated amateurs use a similar process. There are good reasons for its use, but it is an elaborate business.

We noticed earlier that the camera lens was less selective than the eye, but it is a miracle of selectivity compared with the microphone. When you are listening to a radio programme you may be disturbed or irritated by external sounds, but except in extreme cases, such as a very noisy motorcycle passing during a soft string passage, your ear will continue to attend to the matter in hand. Not so the microphone, which will record with amiable indifference any sound within its range. It cannot pay attention to a specific thread of sound, as you do. Consequently, if you make a recording of a radio programme through a microphone at your usual listening distance, you will find that you have also recorded the dog chewing biscuits, doors slamming, taps running and perhaps somebody next door mowing the lawn. (This is one reason why you tape radio programmes direct, and not through a microphone. The other reason is that the microphones associated with small tape recorders are not of very high quality, though they are normally as good as the recorders need.)

This effect is compounded by the automatic level control. Unfortunately, since its basic function is to level out the volume of sound recorded, it also amplifies distant noise when there is none nearby. I have a recording of birds singing in the garden that at one point includes the lowing of a cow a quarter of a mile away. In the context it doesn't matter, and to give the gadget its due it did pick up the birdsong, which might well have been missed if I had had to fiddle with levels. But if the distant sound had been klaxons or a fire alarm that bit would have been ruined.

Nevertheless, without some such automatic arrangement the integrated system would not work at all. It is impossible for one person to look through the viewfinder and watch sound levels at the same time, and you can't have two on the job because there is only one piece of machinery. If you are working on coupled tape, though, it is possible to have a friend to operate the recorder, control the levels and so minimise the unwanted sound.

You will have noticed that television producers, both of extempore interviews and of discussion programmes, get over the confusion of sound by holding microphones close to people's mouths or hanging them round their necks. They would not do this if there were any reasonable alternative, and we are not likely to do any better than they can. So it is instructive to make a dummy tape on a cassette recorder to find out what you do get back.

You might record through the microphone a musical programme from the radio, and make other trial tapes in the garden, on the beach or in the park. Or, instead of recording, you could listen through a pair of headphones attached to the camera, to hear just what sounds are picked up in a variety of situations. You will probably find that recordings made in the house can be adequate, provided that you choose a quiet time of day, shut all the windows and doors and gain the silence of all those not directly concerned. But try it with a camera running too, to see how much motor noise you pick up. Outside, you will find some effective scenes in which sound plays a predominant part – marching bands, performances of songs and dances where the audience is paying attention, or even speeches if they form part of your plan. However, when the sound is incidental rather than essential – of traffic in the street, or children on the sand – results may be less than satisfactory. Sometimes you may be able to use them, other times not. You are never likely to produce triumphs of the art of recording, but then that is not what you are aiming at; you simply want the atmosphere of the occasion.

We are left, then, with the position that our sound camera cannot produce useful or acceptable sound for the whole of our film. It will work only where suitable sounds were predominant. Unless we are prepared to put up with sections of silence or of indeterminate noise, we must do as professionals do: add linking sound afterwards to our recording. There is no great difficulty about this, though it does require thought and patience. And we have the consolation that magnetic sound can be erased and replaced if it is unsatisfactory.

Planning sound films

The process of planning sound films is not very different from that for silent ones, except that sound annotations must be added. It will be possible to predict – after a little experience – which sequences will benefit from live sound and which will need to be covered by commentary and background music. But, provided that your apparatus is sufficiently flexible, it is always better to record as much live sound as possible and replace the unsatisfactory bits later if necessary.

Start, then, as before, with your framework, but add a second column for sound notes. Clearly, if you are making a holiday film of a place you don't already know, the sound notes will be incomplete. So keep your notebook with you, and add remarks as you film.

When you do get good live sound, you can hold your shots for much longer than you could for a silent sequence. The sound will hold your audience, and it is only logical to go on until the band – shall we say – marches out of earshot. Indeed, it is positively distracting if they are cut off in the middle of a bar for no apparent reason.

Technically, too, if you are recording or projecting with a coupled tape recorder, the electronics get confused by very short bursts of sound, and this can cause trouble when

136

playing back. Electric impulses act very quickly, but the machinery they control takes a little time to obey. You cannot expect a recording machine to start, stop and start again within a few seconds, though it will try its best.

Editing sound films

Good editing makes even more difference to sound films than to silent ones. Of course, the job has to be done at least twice. You start by editing the pictures, and then sort the sound out to fit. To do this, except in the most primitive way,

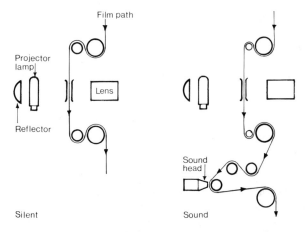

The film passes through the projection gate in a jerky intermittent movement. This must be smoothed completely before it passes the sound head on a magnetic-sound projector or camera

you need more equipment than the basic sound camera and projector. Your projector should be able to record as well as play back. You also need a sound editing machine, so that you can detect where the first sound and the last image occur (see below), otherwise your cutting is likely to go astray.

Editing live Super 8 sound

The sound on a film is not recorded opposite the relevant picture, but (in Super 8) 18 frames ahead. The reason for this is that the film has to stop momentarily as each frame passes the lens, a film being a series of still photographs shown very quickly one after the other. But magnetic stripe has to pass smoothly across the playing head, or the sound would be horrible. Consequently the sound head is at such a distance from the picture gate as to allow the film to pass it smoothly. As a result, if you edit your film as you would a silent one, you get odd bits of sound in the wrong places – or worse, one-second bursts of gaping mouths saying nothing.

Some early sound cameras need a little time to 'warm up', so they record nothing for the first second or so of a shot. Most, though, now have a first-pressure setting on the trigger. This allows the automatic exposure system to operate, and it lets you check the viewfinder signals to see that everything is fine. At the same time the sound system warms up, ready to record as soon as the film starts moving.

If you can be quite sure that you will use two scenes together, you can record the sound of the second straight after that of the first. If you are expecting to edit, though, it is important to ensure that important sounds start at least one second after the picture. For the greatest flexibility, try to begin shooting with some nondescript background sounds (or, better, an appropriate silence) that should not sound too out of place on the beginning of another scene.

Even with modern arrangements for warming up, sound recording often reaches full volume a few frames after visual, so there is a gap between the end of one sound sequence and the beginning of the next. The few intervening visual frames can be cut out, thus reducing the confusion at the change of sequence.

In simple stripe-sound editing you cut your film at the first sound and then at the last picture, and so on throughout the film. The results will not be perfect, but they will be adequate for a start.

All you need to do is bear in mind the way the system works. When you cut off the previous piece of film you remove 18 frames (one second's worth at 18 fps) of sound from the beginning of a scene. When you splice on another shot, you add 18 frames of sound (belonging to whatever originally followed that shot) to the beginning.

There have been proposed a number of gadgets to transfer the sound from its normal position to a position alongside the relevant pictures, then to return it 18 frames ahead after editing. This is fine in theory, but it involves two stripe-to-stripe transfers, which must reduce the quality. It also involves tinkering with your precious original sound, which you cannot replace. So, unless you are making sophisticated drama movies, it is much better to film in a way that ensures easy editing.

Adding extra sound
When you have edited your film, you will probably find yourself with some good sound, some not so good or even pointless, and some silent sequences. As before, run through under normal showing conditions, timing both the sound sections and the gaps. Note the subjects, and arrange additional sound effects or music and commentary. Then gather your material and feed it in, by whatever method you have chosen, to the gaps on the track.

With a single-track stripe projector, this calls for care and dexterity. It will be necessary to run the projector on 'play' for the pieces already recorded, and then switch over to 'record' for the additional material, and so on through the film. Each new section should be a little shorter than the gap: a second or so of silence is not important, but you must avoid erasing pieces of the live sound. Smooth switching is also needed, to avoid both switch noise and sudden burst of sound. Probably you will fade in and out, but try not to overdo it. A 'superimpose' or 'mix in' control makes this process easier, but still leaves your live sound vulnerable.

Adding new material, however, is vastly easier if you have a twin-track projector, which can record on the 'balance' stripe as well as on the normal one. Though rather thinner, and somewhat variable, the balance stripe can normally accommodate both music and commentary. With a twin-track projector you can record and perfect your post-process sound on the balance stripe, without disturbing your synchronised live sound on the main stripe. All you have to do with that is to erase any portions you don't need – obviously a less hazardous operation than fitting in segments of new material on the live-sound track.

Some twin-track projectors have twin amplifiers and can give you full stereo reproduction. Obviously if you want to use the facility you have to record on both tracks of the film (in the projector), in which case your new material once again threatens the live sound. However, you have a second problem: while the new material comes out as stereo sound, the synchronised material is confined to one channel. So it is much better to stick to monophonic reproduction (using both tracks, of course) when adding to a soundtrack on a stereophonic projector. Save the stereo function for making complete soundtracks for films shot silent or with wild sound.

A few – highly expensive – sets of camera equipment can record sound on either stripe or separate tape at will, and have ancillary devices that allow transfer, automatically synchronised, between stripe and tape and back again, in addition to post-recording. These offer a comparatively simple solution to the problems of dubbing and editing, but in view of their price are strictly for the devotee.

In some ways recording on pulse tape is simpler than directly on to stripe. In the first place you are not troubled by the one-second sound/vision separation that is an essential feature of stripe, and in the second you can record all the additional material separately, and physically splice it into the live recorded tape, which will not have run while you were taking silent shots. Unsatisfactory bits of live tape can either be re-recorded or removed and replaced, and overlong pieces of either type of material can be simply cut out.

Although double-system sound has advantages at the editing stage, playing it back has all the disadvantages. The electronics are simple in themselves, but they have to be translated into effects. It takes time for relays and motors to

140

react, especially when signals follow one another very quickly. So if you edit tiny snatches into the film, the machinery may fail to respond. In general, try to make each section last at least ten seconds.

Much better, therefore, is to record your finished sound-track on to a stripe on your film, then replay it in a stripe sound projector.

Sound recording and editing processes are really much more difficult to describe than to carry out, particularly since there are varying systems. Taken a step at a time they are comparatively simple in practice, though they do need leisure as well as care and attention. The results are proportionately satisfying and effective.

10

The apparatus for you

Before reviewing the range of equipment currently available, I should disclose my own views about design, so that those who do not share them are duly forewarned. In brief, I think that automatic operation has gone too far – so far, indeed, that quite a large proportion of this book, which is supposed to be about taking pictures, has had to be devoted to explaining how to fool the automatic devices in order to get the result you want.

Automatic exposure control produces the right results for most of the time, but if it breaks down there may be no way of using the camera until it is repaired. Even manual override may be no help; the aperture control and readout can depend on correctly-functioning automatics. I can see no particular virtue in a motor-driven zoom; hand operation is just as easy, much quicker and avoids the need for one more possible cause of expensive trouble.

An older camera I possess has an exposure meter coupled to the aperture ring with a display in the viewfinder; it can be set through the viewfinder window for the recommended aperture, one stop higher or one stop lower. Any further adjustments can be made by looking at the aperture ring on which the stops are marked, and if the meter breaks down you can use a separate one. This sort of system needs a little more initial mastery, but can cope with a wider range of situations without recourse to special techniques. I would prefer to see this as the basic type of cine camera. However, automatic exposure is now universal, and we have to pay extra if we want to be able to override the camera's opinions.

Shooting the film

Cameras
Camera lenses are complicated, zoom lenses especially so. They are composed of many differently ground pieces of glass. Very broadly, the choice of the glass for these elements, and the precision of their grinding and assembly, determine the quality of the image. Often the number of elements is quoted, but with modern design methods lenses of the same focal-length range and maximum aperture now all have virtually the same number of elements.

In theory, a top-quality lens will always produce sharper pictures than one of less good provenance. However, the difference today is mainly one of quality control. If you buy a camera with a really expensive lens from a respected maker, you can be assured that the quality control has been of the highest, whereas if you buy a camera of apparently the same specification for half the price, you are taking a chance: it may be superb, or it may be below acceptable standard.

A wide variety of lens and shutter control options are available, the most common of which are the following.
(a) *Fixed focus, automatic exposure.* Very basic: the cine equivalent of a box Brownie or, in more modern terms, of the cheaper cartridge-loading cameras. Rather limited in its range, but within its limits perfectly effective. Few are now available.
(b) *Focusing lens, automatic exposure.* Much the same as (a), but allows sharper definition at close ranges, and closer shots. Cameras of this type are virtually unknown today, when virtually all cine cameras have zoom lenses.
(c) *Non-focusing zoom lens, automatic exposure.* The simplest cameras commonly available. Short zoom range ($2 \times$ or $3 \times$) allows reasonably close focus even at longest-focal-length setting. Coupling focus to aperture (incorrectly called servofocus) ensures the maximum use of depth of field at the 'wide' end. This needs special

143

care to keep the subject far enough away at the 'tele' end.

(d) *Focusing zoom lens, automatic exposure.* Much more versatile. Lens usually of large aperture (about $f/1.8$), allowing use in darker conditions. Longer-range zoom allows you to frame the picture you want even though you cannot, or may not wish to, move your own position. In assessing, pay attention particularly to the range of focal lengths provided by the lens, often expressed in terms of magnification, but based on the minimum length available. For instance a 1:4 zoom might work between 8 mm and 32 mm – probably the most likely range – or between 6 mm and 24 mm. Zooms are available in ranges from as little as 1:2½, 10–25 mm, to as much as 1:10, 6.5–65 mm or more, with a corresponding spectrum of cost. Any range is useful, and 8 mm to 48 mm or thereabouts is more than adequate for most purposes. Most zooms offer motor control, but this is not essential, even for sophisticated film making.

(e) *XL cameras.* In 1971 Kodak introduced the first XL camera, intended to be capable of working in normal interior lighting. To achieve this, they combined three factors: 160 ASA film (instead of 40 ASA), a true $f/1.2$ lens with no meter or viewing take-off (instead of the effective $f/2.4$ or so of most then-current reflex models) and a 220° shutter angle (instead of the more normal 160–180°). Together these modifications added up to a minimum light requirement of at least four stops less than previously needed. That is, the camera produced fully exposed images with one-sixteenth of the light. For static subjects it could be set to nine frames per second to gain yet another stop. Since then, the other manufacturers have included XL features in most of their cameras. The simplest, of course, is to accept 160 ASA film. Coupled with 220–230° shutters and $f/1.2$ zoom lenses, even with viewing and metering losses this allows you to film in bright home conditions, day or night. There is no doubt that XL cameras will produce results in conditions only recently considered impossible.

(f) *Automatic exposure with some control.* 'Backlight control' gives about double the exposure if the background is light and the main subject in the foreground is dark; also useful for dull weather. 'Lighting control' gives both a backlight control, as above, and a second position giving half the average exposure if the subject is very bright against a dark background. Both very useful.

(g) *Optional manual exposure.* Allows the operator to select the aperture. Not often necessary, but occasionally very useful for problem shots. A reading is taken (either with a separate meter or with the camera set to 'automatic') from a position in which only the item of principal interest is included – right up against the cathedral window from inside, for instance. The camera is then set to 'manual' and to the same aperture reading. If it is impossible to get right up to the object itself, the exposure can be read from a similar subject in similar lighting: one's hand in shadow will do duty for a shadowed face. A direct reading may be possible if the zoom range is long enough. Essential for using filters if the light meter does not work through the lens.

(h) *Automatic focusing.* See page 40. In the right conditions, keeps your principal subject in focus at any distance to within about 1½ metres (5 feet) of the lens, wherever it moves. Before buying, examine the specification very carefully to see the limits within which the device works.

(i) *Macro focusing.* This is a fancy name for extremely close photography. You can fill your screen with a magnified butterfly. Amusing occasionally; you must decide whether you need it. Probably one of those devices that only specialists – entomologists for instance – will use very often. Most normal lenses will bring you close enough for titling, which is desirable.

(j) *Single-frame photography.* Essential for cartoon work, and helpful in some types of titling. If your camera has it, so much the better.

(k) *Variable filming speeds.* Except for one or two specialised purposes, such as reproduction through a television set or a TV scanning device, the uses of film speeds other than the standard 18 or 24 frames per second for better sound quality are limited, bearing in mind that it is not possible to vary projection speed for different parts of the same film. A slow-motion speed of 36 or 54 frames per second is occasionally amusing and sometimes useful, but this can often be obtained on cameras offering no other speed changes. Nine frames per second can be used to produce results in unusually dark places provided, and only provided, that nothing moves. 24 frames per second can be used as a standard rate for sound films, so that the reproduction of sound benefits from the higher 'tape' speed. But this also uses more film for the same projection time than does 18 frames per second, and so costs you more.

Sound cameras
Stripe (integrated or sound-on-film) sound facilities are available in conjunction with any optical specification. Double-sound (i.e. synchronised tape) systems, in spite of their advantages, are not now widely available, though at least one manufacturer does offer both facilities.

Surprisingly, the sound quality of all but the cheapest models is more or less the same. One quite reputable camera manufacturer claims that his camera has wow and flutter (distortion caused by slight irregularities in tape speed and contact with the recording/playing head) of *only* 1 per cent, whereas even for low-cost tape recorders makers claim figures of 0.2 per cent and less. Figures in the 1 per cent region tend to suggest quite audible fluctuation, though it depends on what you are recording and how good your ear is.

Much in sound work will in the end depend on the facilities in your projector for superimposing and re-recording. There is always in my mind the insidious thought that unless you really need exact synchronisation between sound and vision you can do quite well with a silent camera, a tape recorder for outside use, and a versatile sound projector for making up the final track. However, that can never quite duplicate the spontaneity generated by a synchronised recording of a toddler's first public words.

My reservations about recording sound directly in the camera are not caused by any doubts about the enhanced effect that sound can give, but by the difficulties in the way. The recording of live sound is now technically a very simple matter (and the extra cost of simple sound facilities is not enormous), but it is fraught with acoustical difficulties. Only if the noise you are recording dominates all other local sound, or if you can get your microphone so close to the source of the sound you want to hear that it dominates all others, are you likely to get an acceptable sound recording. Sometimes this is possible, sometimes not.

When buying equipment, consider whether you really want live sound and are going to take the trouble to edit it, or whether perhaps you will be satisfied with post-synchronised tracks of suitable sounds – or even with plain silent films, however much less satisfactory they may be.

Additional facilities

A number of additional facilities, offered on the more expensive cameras, have been left out of account in this review, partly because you get most of them willy-nilly if you buy the most advanced models, and partly because some of them seem to me to be so remote from practical life that they are unlikely ever to be used.

In the former class come fade and dissolve facilities, which can be very useful provided that you can see when a fade is indicated, or your photography is so well organised that the sequence you want to dissolve into follows immediately upon the sequence you want to dissolve out of.

Radio remote control is banned in the UK; it may come in handy when the camera operator wants to appear in his own picture and can't find anyone else to press the button for him, but otherwise the uses seem to me to be as remote as the control. Similarly, some sound cameras have sockets to which you can attach an external sound source. Clearly, if you intend to film performers who use amplified sound

147

(whether live or recorded), a direct camera input will give you better sound quality than will the microphone.

The choice of a camera

Cameras are like most other things: very broadly you get what you pay for. It is wise to remember that quite a lot of the cost of the more expensive cameras goes in quality control – in checking that every bit of the machine is up to the standards set by the makers. I once bought a fairly cheap still camera that gave me such excellent results that an acquaintance bought an apparent duplicate. His results were so poor that he returned it and got something else. This disparity would not have occurred had we both bought, say, Leicas.

Also, a considerable proportion of the cost goes in making the machinery robust. Not long ago I was talking to a professional photographer who commented that I was likely to get excellent results from a fairly newly acquired (still) camera, since he had been using several in his work. However, he was trading in his own and buying a different make with a very similar specification at about three times the cost. When I asked him why, he pointed out that his cameras took two or three hundred shots a day, and the cheaper variety did not stand the wear and tear. It would, though, last a lifetime in my hands, since I was unlikely to take as many as three hundred shots a month.

Cameras in the lowest price range for their specification may be uneven in their performance, though none sold by a reputable dealer should be anything but reliable, and if they can be shown to be faulty the dealer will normally replace them. The most expensive, on the other hand, are very durable as well as very reliable, and can in some cases be tougher than the buyer really needs.

The use to which the camera will be put, and the amount of use it will get, affects the range in which the choice is made: perfectly effective films can be made with very simple apparatus, and it is not worth paying for facilities that are never going to be used. For fairly casual family photography therefore, and particularly for people with little photographic experience, I would recommend a simple straightforward

148

camera with a modest zoom lens. Certainly a beginner is well advised to start with modest though sturdy equipment. If he finds the need for more elaborate equipment he can always exchange it later, at little loss if he has bought well in the first place.

Filters

Filters are optional extras. There may be some benefit in having a skylight filter permanently in position over the camera lens; others should be acquired when experience shows the need. However, if you are likely to make a great deal of use of high-speed films, a neutral-density filter of either $2\times$ or $4\times$ may be necessary in sunshine.

Camera supports

Any movement of the camera shows up as a wavering image on the screen. The longer the focal length of the lens in use, the greater the movement you see on the screen. We put up with these horrid shivers, but for the best results a camera support is more than merely desirable. There are a number of types available:

● *Tripod.* A good tripod is undoubtedly the firmest and best type of support, but it has to be a good one. A flimsy tripod is a false friend; it simply adds its own shakes to those of your hands. A tripod should be fairly heavy, or the weight of the camera and the vibration of the shutter will set it moving on its own account. Consequently it is a piece of apparatus that many amateurs prefer not to use, because of its conspicuousness and its weight. But it is invaluable, especially for close shots and for those at maximum focal length. A tripod should be equipped with at least a ball-and-socket head so that the camera angle can be adjusted in relation to the tripod itself, and preferably with a 'pan and tilt' head so that the camera can be aimed in different directions at lower or higher angles as required.
● *Rifle or shoulder grip.* An arm that screws on to the camera and extends backwards to the shoulder piece, so that you can aim as you would with a rifle. Light and easily portable, at least in the simpler forms.

● *Monopod.* A single telescopic rod, screwing into the camera and reaching the ground, also known as a unipod. Of less use with cine cameras, which have eye-level viewfinders, than with waist-level viewfinder still cameras.

● *Neckstrap.* Downward pressure against a strap round the neck can provide a degree of steadiness. Definitely better than nothing.

Shaping the film

Splicers

Anyone without a splicer is condemned forever to show 50 foot (15 metre) lengths of film exactly as they come back from processing, or perhaps groups of four 50 foot lengths joined together by a commercial processor. You need a splicer even if only for the elementary purpose of cutting out the bad frames – there are always some – and making up lengths of film that last more than three and a bit minutes without a break.

There are broadly two sorts. One cuts the film so that the two ends to be joined butt together and are then wrapped in a plastic tape bandage; the other makes an overlapping joint and provides for scraping the emulsion from one of the two pieces, which are then welded together with an acetate solvent-type cement. The former is said be be quicker, though I find the bits of tape awkward to handle. The resulting joints are strong, but sometimes show on the screen. The latter type is used for professional films, and there are sophisticated models with motors that produce beautiful bevelled joints. They are for perfectionists; the ordinary hand-operated sort works perfectly well, though the joints do occasionally dry out and snap. However, films on polyester base (which includes all Single 8 films) must be joined by tape.

Editor–viewers

An editor–viewer is just about essential for making attractive films. Its purpose is described in Chapter 6, but briefly it allows the film to be reviewed frame by frame where necessary, and provides for marking places for cutting,

150

whether to remove bad bits or to reorganise the order. The good parts can be moved on very quickly so as to reach the pieces that need attention. It has two spool holders and a small illuminated screen. In its simplest form it is entirely hand operated, but more advanced models are motor driven. There are special types for sound, so that the soundtrack can be heard, and very special ones with sound erasing and recording facilities so that the soundtrack can be made up on the editor instead of on the projector.

You can try to edit without an editor–viewer if you wish, but in the end you will find that you need one. If other ways of dealing with sound are available (or if sound is not a factor) probably the simplest model is best, so long as it produces a good clear image and does not scratch the film.

Titling equipment
Although many titles and subtitles can be produced without it, some sort of special equipment is extremely useful for giving a polish to the film. Options available include:

● Letter sets and backgrounds of felt, metal or plastic. These can be used without other equipment, provided that some means is available of holding the camera quite still, such as a sufficiently adaptable tripod.
● Titling easels with camera stands. These make the use of letter sets and other materials easier, provided that they are compatible with the focusing limits of the camera. Rarely needed nowadays when most cameras are zoom reflex types.
● More complicated – and expensive – arrangements help to make moving as well as still titles and provide for a wide variety of title treatment. This is equipment for the enthusiast.

Showing the film

Projectors
The first decision to be made concerns the quality and capabilities of the projector to be bought. The quality should be the highest practicable, of course; see later. If you have a stock of older Double 8 films, you will need a projector that

takes Double 8 as well as Super 8. Whether or not you require this adaptability, you will wish to consider whether to buy a silent or a stripe-sound projector. A stripe projector provides much the simplest way of reproducing sound films. If you choose – and it is a very valid choice – to film entirely without camera-recorded sound, you can record commentary and background music on stripe. If you choose to record sound on the camera, again you need a stripe projector. If you prefer to use the 'double system' of camera coupled to tape recorder, you can re-record the live sound on to the stripe and have the simplicity of stripe projection with the sound in exact synchronisation with the film.

It will take a considerable amount of dexterity and experience to get live soundtracks into exact synchronisation, but it can be done; even if they are marginally out, the difference is not going to attract much attention. You will get more accurate synchronisation with a double-system projector, but against this you have to balance the fact that what you put on stripe sticks for ever, whereas with other systems there can be mechanical or electrical failures. Moreover, every stripe film can be played on every stripe projector, whereas double systems are not so adaptable.

The choice of system having been made, it is essential that editing facilities are available. With sound on separate tape, this would be a function of the recorder; with integrated sound, provision must be made somewhere else. This can be in the projector, which may be the simplest solution. But it can also be in the sound editor, though this is probably a more expensive alternative. Go for a projector, in this case, that can erase, record and superimpose sound on the film, as almost all do.

You might well come to the conclusion – and it would be a perfectly valid one – that, whatever recording system you adopt, the final projection will be from stripe. In this case you should consider whether record/play facilities on main stripe only are adequate, or whether you would prefer to have available the greater flexibility allowed by the ability to record on the second (balance) stripe. As detailed in Chapter 9, a twin-track projector is highly desirable if you want to include much in-camera recorded sound. It allows you to work on the second stripe, thus preventing accidental erasure of irreplaceable material on the main stripe. Then comes the question of stereophonic recording. This is virtually confined to post-synchronised work. But if you intend to make soundtracks for films shot in silence, it is well worth considering.

It pays to buy a good projector. The film goes through the camera only once, but through the projector many times. Any roughness, any irregularity in the film path will slowly – and sometimes not so slowly – destroy your records of the past, so precision engineering is a necessity. Further, it is essential that the film gate, in addition to being faultlessly smooth, should hold the film exactly flat for the instant of projection. If it does not, the image on the screen will not be sharp all over. It might seem that these two points would be basic considerations for all makers; no doubt they are, but not all achieve equally successful results.

Other points of variation between models are:

• The sharpness of the image on the screen. This depends mainly on the quality of the lens; in cheaper models there can be variation between one individual lens and the next.
• The illumination of the image. This depends for its evenness on the whole optical system, and for its brightness on the performance of the lamp. Sometimes the lamp or the mirror can be adjusted for evenness, but if a projector cannot illuminate evenly, adjustable or non-adjustable, it should be rejected. The light output of all but the cheapest projectors currently available is surprisingly similar. The main factor in image brightness is the aperture of the lens. For home viewing it is better to select a sharp lens of more modest aperture than a wider-aperture lens of lower quality.
• The stability of the focus. Every projector should have a positive focusing mechanism, without backlash and stable during projection. One would think that this would be provided in all reputable projectors, but unfortunately, in my experience, it is not. In particular, projectors with fiddly focusing systems that react to tiny movements of the control should be avoided.

153

- Fixed or zoom lens. With a fixed lens you have to move the projector backwards and forwards to fit the image to the screen; the zoom lens, within limits, avoids this necessity. The zoom is useful but not essential, especially if projector and screen are always going to be roughly in the same places.
- Spool sizes accepted. Any reasonable projector ought to accept at least 400-foot (120 metre) spools, which last half an hour or a little less. A few are limited to 200 feet, which to me at least seems too little. In fact it is unusual to find a good-quality projector that will not take 400 foot spools. Most now accept even longer ones, particularly sound projectors, which take 600, 800 or sometimes even 1200 foot spools. Remember than stripe takes up extra space, so a 600 foot reel is needed to accommodate a generous 400 feet of striped film.
- Adaptability between Super 8 and the older Standard 8. Many silent projectors offer this feature, as do a few sound ones, although the latter are rapidly going off the market. Anyone who is likely to need this facility would be well advised to snap up a sample smartly – remembering that Standard 8 films can be striped for background music and commentary. Some dual models adapt at the pressure of a switch; this seems simple, but in fact the results on the screen may be nowhere near as good as with machines that require a physical change of gates and sprockets.
- Television-type screens. Some projectors now available can project either on a normal screen or, with the aid of a couple of mirrors, on a piece of opal plastic about the size of a television screen. The image is visible in daylight, and is very suitable indeed for a family audience. The idea is not new: a gadget called a daylight screen on exactly the same principle has been in use for many years, and I once made one myself with the aid of a few bits of plywood and the necessary glassware. But those available on the market are neat and unobtrusive. By no means essential, but very useful.

Never buy a projector without seeing a demonstration, and for preference a comparative demonstration of two or three projectors, using the same film each time. The final selection should be made on the basis of this performance, bearing in mind the money available and the purposes for which the projector is to be used. There is no point in buying one that would be adequate for a small hall if it is only to be used at home, but on the other hand it is foolish to have carefully constructed films debased by poor reproduction or damaged by poor machinery. And of course if you buy well in the first place there will be no need to replace the projector simply because you get a better camera.

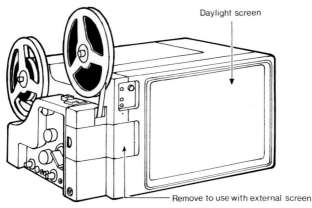

Daylight screen

Remove to use with external screen

Instead of a normal projector and screen, a television-like daylight projector is ideal for home viewing. Most can also throw an image on to a normal screen

Camera and projector are the two basic elements of the outfit. The most expensive equipment can cost ten times as much as the cheapest, so it pays to select carefully and ensure that whatever is bought represents good value for money. Apart from anything else, there are other items needed to a greater or lesser extent, as has already been indicated.

Screens

A film can be shown on a matt white wall, if one is available in the right place and if the surface is reasonably even. Failing that, a large piece of matt white paper, such as cartridge paper, will do if it can be made to stay upright. A sheet, however, is not usually an adequate substitute for a screen, because it is rarely possible to persuade it to hang without wrinkles and because its reflecting capacity is even more limited than a wall or paper: of course the light from the projector must be reflected back to the eyes of each viewer. A glossy surface, on the other hand, is never suitable because it reflects blotches of light unevenly and the picture is not clearly visible.

Better than any of these is a screen designed for the purpose, preferably one that matches the size of picture you wish to see. Portable screens are all provided with stretchers – so that their surfaces lie flat and unwrinkled – and are designed variously to hang from hooks, to stand on tables, or to be supported on their own tripod stands. The last type is often the most convenient, and second to them the hanging sort. The cheapest table-standing screens are often slightly less effective because, for stability, they tilt backwards, which creates problems in focusing and in getting the picture square; the better ones will stand squarely upright on a solid base.

Ideally, the projector should be exactly opposite the middle of the screen, with the film gate exactly parallel to the projection surface. There is a certain amount of tolerance, but any great divergence from the ideal produces a picture with the sides slanting outwards at the top if the projector is lower than the screen, or at the bottom if it is higher. The former is the more usual trouble, and it is exaggerated if the screen itself slopes away from the projector at the top.

Screens are available with matt white, beaded or lenticular surfaces. The matt surface produces the best widespread image and is equally bright from any angle of view. It is the best type for a normal small audience. The beaded surface reflects a very bright image straight back to the projector position, but the brightness falls off rapidly as the viewer moves to either side. The lenticular screen has tiny, slightly curved vertical stripes, and is designed to produce a brighter image than a matt surface without such a rapid rate of deterioration as with the beaded screen, but it is at best rather less bright than the latter.

156

The reason why it is best to have a screen the same size as the proposed picture, and not larger, is that the better screens have a black edge. If the image is projected just a fraction larger than the white area, the tiny scraps of dust that always collect round the projection gate will be masked by the black surround, so the projected image will have clean edges instead of the untidy fringe that is otherwise inevitable.

Projector stands

Projectors often have to stand on piles of books to raise them to approximately the right level, and even then have to be tilted excessively by means of adjustable front feet to enable the image to reach even what seems to be a comparatively low screen. While by no means essential, projector stands save a lot of fiddling about and are comparatively cheap. You don't know what a relief they can be until you have tried both methods of support.

Summary

The following you need for a basic outfit:

1. *Camera.* You are likely to be much happier with the best model with simple features than with a similarly priced, cheaply-made, feature-laden model. If you want just to record family, friends, events and places a fixed-focus non-zoom is available. This performs a function equivalent to an automatic compact 35 mm camera. You can do a lot more with it than might be immediately apparent – and it has no complications to intrude on film making. An XL model offers lots of opportunities in the home.

For those more interested in photographic technique there is the camera with a zoom lens of about 3:1 ratio and a backlight control. Once again, think about low-light filming.

Think carefully whether you need a sound camera. For family events it is an enormous boon. If possible, though, try one out first: sound recording is far more difficult to perfect than is basic film making.

For the technically committed there are various other facilities. Each has its use, and you should try to predict your future film making to decide whether you need close-focus capability, a long-range zoom, manual control, variable film speeds and so forth.

2. *Projector.* Again, select the best you can in the class you choose. The class depends on the likely use: in a small room, or occasionally in a large hall? Do you want a conventional screen, or a television-like back-projection unit? The answers are yours. Whether or not you are proposing to record live sound, you may sooner or later want to make background soundtracks or to show commercial sound films. So it might well be worth buying a sound projector in the first place, preferably with recording facilities, and even better with twin-track recording.

3. *Screen.* Type according to needs; size according to the space available. Matt white is best for most purposes. Remember that over-large screens give dull pictures, because the same amount of light is spread over a large area.

4. *Splicer.* A simple hand-operated machine is good enough for most purposes, and cement is preferable to tape unless you are a user of polyester-based films, such as Single 8, which won't stick with cement.

5. *Editor–viewer.* Any model that gives a clear picture and works smoothly will do. A sound editor is useful if you are going to use much live sound, but not essential if you can count up to 18. Extra facilities can be purchased according to taste and purse.

The following can be very useful indeed:

6. *Camera support.* A stout *and firm* tripod will give you steady pictures. It is very desirable for giving a professional steadiness to your normal shots, and essential for longer-range zoom sequences.

7. *Titling aids.* Letters and so on essential for the final polish.

8. *Filters.* As required according to experience. Very advisable as permanent assets are: (a) Skylight filter for dull weather and occasions when there is an excess of blue light, and (b) $2\times$ or $4\times$ neutral density filters for use with fast film in bright sun.

With a silent camera and a tape recorder, you can record both the sights and the sounds of any situation. If the tape is pulsed, you can reproduce the sounds in exact synchronisation. This is wonderful, but not essential; in many circumstances a general impression of the ambient sound is sufficient. Only when you are dealing with a soloist do you really need to match sound exactly to gesture. Generally speaking, an approximation is just as acceptable as a strictly lip-synchronised sequence – though I should not wish to discourage anyone who wishes to go for full reality and is willing to spend the time and energy needed to achieve it. If you choose a sound camera, to record those pieces you would like synchronised, you may find a portable tape recorder a boon as well. Then a second person can concentrate on recording the sound when exact synchronisation is unnecessary.

Such an approximation can be achieved comparatively easily by a combination of film and loosely synchronised tapes. With real care the synchronisation can become exact – and indeed, this is exactly how professionals work. Therefore it is reasonable to consider the possibility of combining a silent camera with a stripe-sound projector and such other accessories as may seem advisable. The stripe-sound projector will ensure that your final film is always synchronised in the way you intended. The resources of the projector and any other apparatus you have available will govern the range of your production, but once your homework is done you will have no further worries, and your film will work on any stripe-sound projector.

In considering these recommendations, you may well need to consider the cost of your operations. Currently, at least, sound film cartridges cost approximately 50% more than silent. Prestriped silent cartridges, on the other hand, cost only marginally more than plain silent ones. The cost of striping existing silent films lies between these two, but of course you do not pay for striping the rejected sequences, and it is said that a complete post-stripe avoids the slight noise made during projection at points where the stripe has been jointed with the film.

Thoughts about assembling your kit

It would be nice if I could round off this section by proposing an ideal starter's outfit. Unfortunately, requirements vary according to the experience and needs of each photographer. However, there are some basic points to consider.

The first concerns the range of subjects you are really going to cover. A camera should cope with all the subjects you really want to photograph, but not be stuffed with facilities you are never going to use. For what one might call garden and beach shots, this would indicate a camera with a fixed-focus or short-range zoom lens and limited XL capacity. But so many new models appear every week that these suggestions can only be related to the date on which they were written. Tomorrow something new might arise. Look, however, for simplicity in operation unless you are prepared to spend much thought in utilising special features. It is wonderful to be able to set up your camera to take a sequence that shows a flower opening, but not very sensible to pay for this facility unless you are actually going to use it.

Secondly, you have to consider whether, and to what extent, you are going to use sound. The simplest way of achieving live sound is a sound-on-film camera. However, although sound enlivens a film beyond recognition, the recording of live sound presents notable difficulties. Is there some compromise that does not require studio facilities or much dedicated work? Leaving on one side the very expensive sets of equipment designed for dedicated enthusiasts only, it seems to me that one possibility exists: the combination of a silent camera – adapted or not for pulsed tape – with a tape recorder and possibly a record player.

Consequently, I would recommend:

● The camera that most nearly matches your present experience.
● A sound camera, if you wish to record live sound in spite of the difficulties.
● In default of the sound camera, a tape recorder, preferably but not entirely necessarily pulse-coupled.
● A stripe-sound projector with as many recording facilities as you desire or can afford.

160

Index